CATERING AND FINANCIAL MANAGEMENT

CATERING AND FINANCIAL MANAGEMENT

PIYUSH BHATNAGAR
SUVARNA SABLE

2007

SBS Publishers & Distributors Pvt. Ltd.
New Delhi

ISBN : 978-81-89741-44-0

Indian Price - Rs 595

First Published in India in 2007

© Reserved

Published by:
SBS PUBLISHERS & DISTRIBUTORS PVT. LTD.
2/9, Ground Floor, Ansari Road, Darya Ganj,
New Delhi - 110002, INDIA
Tel: 23289119, 41563911
Email: mail@sbspublishers.com
www.sbspublishers.com

Printed at Chaman Enterprises, New Delhi.

Preface

Catering management is the art of providing food and drink aesthetically and scientifically to a large number of people in a satisfactory and cost effective manner. Management can be defined as the art of bringing together available resources including the abilities of different people and organizing them in a scientific and orderly manner, to achieve the desired goals of the organization, while promoting individual aspirations as well. In its simplest form, management is the process by which people work together to achieve common goals. It is, however, a continuous process of establishing objectives, putting together all available human and material resources in the best possible manner, in an atmosphere of cooperation and goodwill.

This book has been written to assist catering establishments. An attempt is made in this book to introduce to the readers the important aspects of Catering and Financial Management. This book covers mainly the area of catering and financial management in hotel industry. The material has been planned in thirteen units that encompass the principles and functions of management in catering in different institutions.

We owe a debt of gratitude to a large number of friends and well-wishers the opinions expressed in this book are entirely ours and we take the responsibility for shortcomings if any.

We express my sincere thanks to our publishers, M/s. SBS Publishers and Distributors, New Delhi and their efficient editorial staff who helped in publishing this book.

Mr. Piyush Bhatnagar
Ms. Suvarna Sable

Contents

CONTENTS

One

Principles and Functions of Catering Management

Introduction

Catering management is the art of providing food and drink aesthetically and scientifically to a large number of people in a satisfactory and cost effective manner.

Since every person eats away from home at sometime or the other, and people have different paying capacity for the same food items, at different times, even a roadside food and beverage stall has the potential to flourish.

What then is the role of management in catering operations if a food service establishment is to fulfill this potential? It is this and many such questions that this unit and those that follow attempt to answer.

Management can be defined as the art of bringing together available resources including the abilities of different people and organizing them in a scientific and orderly manner, to achieve the desired goals of the organization, while promoting individual

1

aspirations as well. In its simplest form, management is the process by which people work together to achieve common goals. It is, however, a continuous process of establishing objectives, putting together all available human and material resources in the best possible manner, in an atmosphere of cooperation and goodwill. As catering involves diverse activities and a variety of products and services, it provides a special challenge to the manager. It has certain characteristics that make it different from other manufacturing and service industries. These are:

- A marked dissimilarity of the principal services offered, such as rooms, food, liquor and tobacco.
- A wide variety of food offered in various service styles to the customer, ranging from biscuits and tea cooked and processed snacks, beverages and meals to organization of complete events.
- The product and service are closely interlinked and cannot be treated in isolation.
- The product offered is not always taken off the shelf and served, but requires further preparation or finishing touches before it can be presented to the customer.
- Products are not easy to standardize, and the same dish varies in its shape, size, colour and nutritive and sensory qualities, from one establishment to another.
- Providing a personal touch to the food is an important selling point in catering.
- The ingredients used in food preparation are perishable to varying degrees and therefore special arrangements for their safe storage are necessary.
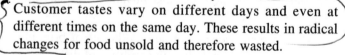
- Customer tastes vary on different days and even at different times on the same day. These results in radical changes for food unsold and therefore wasted.
- Food production can make use of equipment to a certain extent but cannot be fully automated. Besides, caterers

have to deal with a lot of people from varying cultural, religious, social and structural backgrounds. This calls for greater skills in food processing and workers management both within and outside the establishment.

- Food is more vulnerable to pilferage, theft, contamination, spoilage and waste. It therefore needs to be strictly controlled at all stages of production and service.
- The product is generally consumed at the point of production, but while some items can be prepared beforehand and held safely, others cannot, and therefore have to be prepared on order. This results in peaks and troughs of activities.
- Customers have to wait for different lengths of time for being served depending on the extent of their orders.
- The caterer has also to concern himself with standards of hygiene and the health of his customers as food once consumed cannot be retrieved. While other products such as soap can always be discarded by the customer if found unsatisfactory, the adverse effects of an infected food can only be felt after it has been consumed.
- A large variety of costs are incurred in different ways by caterers of different types of services.
- Fixed costs continue to be incurred whether the facilities are used or not.
- The demands of customers vary in the combinations of services required to which caterers have to adjust. For example overnight board, lodging or conference guests, agency custom, restaurant and bar sales to non-residents and banquets. All these give rise to a variety of prices for the same commodity.
- A constant need to price competitively and to know the costs involved in providing products and services profitably.
- There is marked prevalence of seasonal trading.
- There is always a possibility of altering the balance

between the principal services sold, either by extending one service at the expense of another, or by overall expansion. For example, conversion of a lounge into a banquet or conference hall or bar. In view of the above special features catering management requires a professional approach backed by special skills, knowledge and vigilance at every stage of production and service.

This unit deals with the basic concepts and functions of catering management, the tools that can be used to achieve goals effectively and how best resources can be put together to make food services viable.

Principles of Catering Management

Management is a process involving activities through which action is initiated and resources used for achievement of a preset goal. Every manager, to help him in the successful management of his establishment, can formulate certain basic guidelines. These guidelines are called principles of management.

George R. Terry has aptly defined principle as "a fundamental statement or truth providing a guide to thought and action." Principles are thus formulated on the basis of past experiences of managers in related situations, through a process of recording mentally or in writing, the effects of decisions taken in the past. Although no situation can be dealt with in exactly the same manner, present decisions can be based on the results of past decisions taken under fairly similar circumstances, depending on the future goals to be achieved. Thus principles are not rigid foolproof rules to be applied for finding solutions to situations, but flexible, practical, consistent, and relevant guidelines for use in similar sets of situations. Principles, therefore, provide a hypothesis for predicting future happenings when they are used with the manager's own judgment of how and when to apply them.

When managers make decisions that have constantly proved wrong, the fault does not lie in the management principles, but in the judgments made when applying them to a particular situation. For example, a catering manager may follow the principle of serving meals strictly between 12.30 p.m. and 2.30 p.m. every day. However, one day there is an unexpected rush of customers, and prepared meals get finished by 2.00 p.m. His judgment can lead to the following actions:

(i)   Close down service at 2.00 p.m. on that day.

(ii)   Quickly use some ready to serve foods held in stock to make up meals and meet the rush.

(iii)   Request staff to make sandwiches and arrange for serving eggs to order for the remaining half hour of the service.

In this manner there can be so many different reactions to a particular situation that it may seem confusing to make a decision. But the principle if applied with value judgment, helps to make decisions easier and more effective. A manager who places greater value on the "goodwill of his customers" will not think twice about keeping the food service open, and providing whatever he can to his customers. He would not take the risk of turning away even a single customer. Another might value his own image vis-a-vis the staff, in which case he will treat the situation as a challenge and think of quick preparations, being guided by the principle of keeping the food service open. A third manager may value good relations with staff and take the opportunity to give them half-an-hour off, based on his decision that the number of customers between 2.00 p.m. and 2.30 p.m. are not significant enough to go through the exercise of preparing meals over again and taxing his staff unduly.

In this manner the number of decisions possible can be as many as the value judgments people have. Principles applied must therefore, be flexible enough to be used in situations where goals change from time to time, no matter how far apart in time similar situations may arise. Principles represent the historical collection of 'cause and effect' data obtained from experiences of managers in various situations, from which practicing and potential managers can draw for making decisions effectively.

There is no fixed number of principles that a manager may adopt as the basis of developing his establishment, and with individual experiences gained, very different guidelines for efficient working may be established in different organizations. Some principles help managers to predict, others provide guidelines for decision-making at various levels of an organization. According to Koontz O 'Donnel and Weihrich, principles in management "are descriptive or predictive, and no prescriptive". In other words, they do not tell a manager what he should do, but only give him an idea of what may be expected if certain variables interact in a situation.

Some principles that form basic guidelines of managing catering operations are:

(a) Division of work;
(b) Authority and responsibility;
(c) Discipline;
(d) Unitary command;
(e) Unitary direction;
(f) Individual goals subordinate to establishment goals;
(g) Payment of remuneration;
(h) Hierarchy;
(i) Orderliness
(j) Loyalty and devotion;
(k) Work stability;
(l) Initiative;
(m) Unity and
(n) Control.

Division of Work

The principle of division of work is based on the concept of specialization, and since food production activities are each quite distinct in the skills they require, jobs are generally divided according to abilities of staff. The idea is to make abilities more efficient by performing each task repeatedly, till production speeds up and staff gains confidence. As the size of the establishment increases the principle of division of work becomes more applicable as against a small coffee shop in which a cook and his assistant do most of the kitchen work, and shift to the service counter when production is over. Similarly, an owner-manager of a small canteen would probably perform the tasks of the cashier, accounts clerk, purchasing manager, recruiting staff, catering supervisor and so on. But as the establishment increases in size and the amount of work increases, the jobs would be delegated to people having the required abilities to handle them.

The principle of division of work, however, has to be applied with care in food services because its strict application might lead to staff being unable to takeover another's job. For example, if a cook leaves, the assistant would not be able to produce the food for the customer, to the detriment of the establishment. The principle should only be applied to the extent to which it helps timely achievement of goals. Since food has to be prepared and served at a particular time, this principle may be used to ensure speed.

Authority and Responsibility

The principle of authority works in two ways, that which is exercised because of position in the organization, through the chain of command formally laid out, and that which is attributed to a person's intelligence, experience and the sense of values he holds. Both types of authority complement each other. In any

7

work situation some of the official authority may be delegated along with the responsibility a task carries. For example, the catering manager to the head chef in the kitchen may delegate the task of meal production and job distribution. He then also gets with the delegated job, the responsibility of ensuring correct portions, standards, quality, customer satisfaction and profits. Authority may also be dispersed or centralized in principle.

Discipline

The principle of discipline covers punctuality, courtesy, adherence to rules and regulations, obedience all of which are essential for smooth functioning of establishments where group activities are involved and directed towards common goals.

Unitary Command

Application of the unitary command principle goes a long way in establishing loyalty to the senior in command and to the organization. It removes chances of confusion and improves communications through better understanding of particular personalities.

Where more than one-person is given different instructions, loyalties get divided and subordinates take advantage of the conflicting situation to evade work. The result is that time gets wasted, work gets disorganized and performance and efficiency drops.

Unitary Direction

This relates to coordination of activities to achieve a single goal. There can be no command without direction. Undirected or multidirectional goals only lead to confusion and unachieved goals.

Individual Goals Subordinate to Establishment Goals

This principle is important for the success of any establishment, because if every individual starts working to achieve his own goals first and then those of the establishment, there is no doubt that the organization will have to close down. This is because there is no end to individual needs and when one is satisfied another will crop up, at the cost of the food service.

Payment or Remuneration

All work must be paid for in order to motivate people to do their best. The methods of payment agreed on should satisfy employees and the organization, the terms in principle being, as far as possible, impartial.

Hierarchy

The principle of hierarchy refers to the chain formed by staff placed at different levels in an organization, and corresponds to the various levels of management line, middle, and top management.

Orderliness

This principle is most applicable to catering establishments that are constantly handling materials, heavy equipment and working with steam and other fuels. Material orderliness is of utmost importance because perishables need to be kept for different periods of time in raw, partly prepared and prepared forms. Orderliness helps to avoid cross-contamination, saves time looking for materials and equipment when required and ensures safety for all concerned.

Orderliness with regard to manpower is helpful in placing people in positions so that "the right man is in the right place at the right time" a reflection of good organization.

Loyalty and Devotion

This principle ensures an atmosphere at work that is bound to generate a unified attachment to the organization and its interests and goals, through development of harmonious relations at work.

Work Stability

The principle of minimized labour turnover creates a sense of security and confidence in people, leading to better orientation at work. If this principle is not followed for any reason, and cheap labour is employed haphazardly, the turnover increases. This is very costly both in terms of the wage bill and increased recruitment and administrative cost, besides resulting in poor performance.

Initiative

If staff is allowed to suggest plans that can be followed even partly, it is highly motivating for them. For example, if a recipe idea offered by an assistant cook is accepted and prepared by the head cook, initiative develops in the staff. Based on this principle, staffs are often encouraged to participate in making decisions that affect them. This helps to raise morale, develop new ideas and increase efficiency.

Unity

This principle emphasizes the spirit of group work, and helps to establish of smooth communications, between people, thus developing healthy team spirit.

Control

This principle suggests that limiting the area of control of a leader or supervisor to cover the work of only five or six people having related jobs brings about greater efficiency. This is often referred to as "the span of control".

Thus, principles used with good judgment enhance the chances of reaching set goals, increase understanding between and with people, help in decision-making and encourage better use of resources. Since all plans of action are based on decisions made within the value structures of managers, principles provide the base from where to start towards goals.

Functions of Management

The functions of management for any catering operation, small or large, are basically the activities that a manager performs to get people to work harmoniously towards organizational goals. These functions are distinctly different from the activities involved in the actual production and service of food in a catering establishment.

Planning

Planning is the continuous process by which a manager scrutinizes past performance, reviews its applicability in the light of environmental changes, internal and external to the organization, and forecasts future trends. He then sets the goals for the establishment and bases its activities towards achieving them. The planning process is generally initiated by an awareness of an opportunity or a problem, which can be foreseen in the future. In the light of forecasts the establishment is scrutinized for its strengths and weaknesses, and new objectives and goals are established on the basis of certain assumptions. These are also referred to as "planning premises" and include forecasts pertaining to technological advancement, economic and social factors, governmental controls, customer attitudes and competitive forces. All planning involves three main steps:

First—gathering information for chalking out broad policies relating to building, standards, finances, staff needs, food service methods, type and number of customers desired. In short, any information for making is a workable scheme.

Second—actually developing a blueprint of the structure, arrangement of spaces and activity details that can be conveniently translated into action from the information collected.

11

Third—setting goals or targets to be achieved in a predetermined period of time. The goals must be related to a fairly accurate forecast of future events, since they cannot be based on absolute certainty.

Planning is thus a mental exercise, the results of which are later transcribed on paper for reference as the activities proceed. It is also a continuous process taking place at all levels of management, helping the activities of the establishment to proceed as realistically as possible towards goals in constantly changing environments.

Catering establishments differ from other organizations basically in the type of goods and services they offer. Food being perishable in nature, and customers temperamental in their attitudes towards food, it becomes important for catering managers to set goals for a relatively short period of time.

This usually covers six months to a year in terms of food production goals. But, goals concerning the type of facility to be offered can be set for longer periods. This is because it is not practical to take up restructuring of premises or changing the type of equipment frequently, as they both require high investment and in any case have longer life spans. The planning for building, equipment, etc. is therefore done for five, ten or even fifteen years.

Goal setting is fundamental to any achievement. Any goal set must be clear to the planner as well as to all those who would be involved in the activities for achieving it. This helps people to know 'why' they are doing 'what' and feel a sense of achievement at the end. Work then becomes purposeful, creative, orderly, productive, cost effective and satisfying for all involved. Apart from benefits to the organization, people benefit too, through better relations with each other, economically through bonuses, personal development by acquiring skills and experience and a sense of belonging to the organization.

Goals in any catering establishment need to be set along a continuum as indicated in table 1.1. Beginning from short-to-long-term goals.

Table 1.1: Goal setting in an establishment

Short-Term	Medium-Term	Long-Term
Noe	1 to 5 years	5 to 1 0 to 1 5years
Plan number of	Gross profit margins	Production targets
Customers	Purchase procedures	Capital
Service		
Patterns	Equipment needs	Labour policy Staff training
Equipment		Diversification
Staff duties	Maintenance Customer	
	staff relations	
Menus Market	Financial statements	Research-
—	Menu extension	Operations
Profits	—	—

It will be observed from table that for achievement of goals set at various points in time different skills are involved, starting from the acquisition, production and service of food to long-term policy-making for profitability. These reflect the different staff levels required in a catering establishment for performance of various jobs. As one travels to the right of the goal continuum the amount of mental effort required in planning, and the risks required to be taken in making decisions for the future, increase. This is because it is more difficult to predict changes that may occur in the environment, in say about five or ten years time, as compared to those in six months or a year. It stands to reason therefore that every goal set needs to be reviewed in the light of changes occurring as the activities proceed towards it.

This should be done clearly enough for all those involved in achieving it, to understand what they have to work towards. It is believed that 80 per cent of the important results desired are achieved through 20 per cent of the total goals set. So if every manager shifts the goals along the continuum and identifies six to ten important ones, these can become the key targets for all activities, for which details and standards for achievement can be chalked out and identified. These when written out clearly and understood by all concerned constitute a "plan". Planning catering operations thus involves stating objectives clearly by:

(i) Forecasting the number of customers accurately.

(ii) Judging expectations of customers through familiarity with their food habits, religious and cultural backgrounds and economic status. In other words it means knowing their purchasing power, timings and manner of eating, and expectations from the food service.

(iii) Determining the margin of profit required to cover all costs taking into account inflationary trends, menu composition, tastes of customers and so on.

(iv) Establishing profit policy (once costs are calculated) in the light of financial constraints like tax requirements, subsidies in the form of free meals to employees or subsidized overheads,

(v) Knowing staff skills for production and service.

Accurate future projections of the above help establishments to lay down general policies that would prove feasible over longer periods of time, especially where factors determine the planning of sites, spaces, and facilities, as these cannot be changed or shifted easily once bought and built due to financial and other constraints.

Every establishment irrespective of its size requires formulating plans of action for its present and future success. Though some managers may consider planning to be a costly exercise requiring lot of time, effort and money, it has certain distinct advantages:

(a) It helps to minimize time-wasting activities, involving waiting for instructions or ingredients because of last

14

minute purchasing, leading to an indefinite cycle of uncertainties of what is to be done next and so on.

(b) It helps to see future possibilities making managers alert to changes in trends that may affect the activities of the department. For example, the change in price of a material will immediately make him think of using substitutes. Again, a noticeable change in tastes of customers can be seen through menus that have been planned and recorded over a period of time. These help to inculcate changes in future plans well in time to eliminate wastage of ingredients through overstocking.

(c) It helps to organize and integrate activities in proper sequences, match jobs to skills and increase overall efficiency by helping to see the inter-relationship of the various activities in the light of total objectives of the organization, and of individuals. When each person's responsibility and the contribution their activities make to the final goal are understood, the staffs also get motivated to bring out their best.

(d) It eliminates confusion if the plan is communicated well to those involved in its implementation.

(e) It provides an important basis for control through budgeting of time, energy, space and money, while forming targets for achievement.

(f) It helps managers at all levels to direct their subordinates effectively towards the goals. With every step forward in the right direction, job satisfaction and confidence develop.

Time spent on planning therefore, is time well spent, provided it is not overdone. It gives an idea of the time that may be spent on planning, by staff at different levels in a catering establishment.

Planning Time of Staff (%)

It will be noticed that the higher the level of management in an organization, the greater is the time spent on planning, the least being at the operative level where it is a matter of only sequencing individual activities distributed through detailed plans of work handed down. So while kitchen staff often have the feeling that managers sit all day in their chairs while they do all the work, it is quite clear that the difference is only in the nature of the work. Managers do more mental work while food production and service staffs do more of physically, put plans into action.

Sometimes, however, managers get so involved in planning that they find little time for supervisory, and other important coordinating and directing functions. This leads to constant effort of trying to catch up with neglected functions and correcting unsupervised wrong actions so that confusion, dissatisfaction and inefficiency result. Too much time spent on planning in thus disruptive as well as costly. In addition, it blocks initiative and creativity of staff, delays work and affects staff relations adversely. Also the higher the planning level the greater is the time lag between setting the goals and measuring performance towards them. For instance a dishwasher's performance can be judged on the spot because the goals are set in the activity area, i.e. the kitchen itself. But, a cook's performance in controlling costs can be assessed only after a day, week or month. This is because the goals for profitability are set at the highest level in the establishment and evaluated long after the cooking is done.

Important areas of planning in catering establishments are planning for premises, functional areas, staff and customers, all of which are discussed in the units that follow.

Organizing

Once the goals have been set and responsibilities of work understood by key staff of departments, each area of the plan needs to be put into practice. In the catering field the key areas of activity revolve around the production cycle, service areas, profit planning and record keeping.

Each department manager then has to translate his plan into clear-cut activities, which are then sequenced in a manner that will result in smooth workflow. The ability to establish such a workflow by proper coordination of activities allotted to staff, according to their abilities is termed as "organizing". It involves demarcating areas of activity and then establishing activity—authority relationships for each worker or a group allotted the particular activities.

Steps in Organizing

    (a) Each activity is broken down into specific action units.

    (b) Each action unit is then allotted to a manageable group of people, and authority delegated to a group leader for task performance.

    (c) Staff are allocated to each action unit and placed in positions according to their skills with levels of authority clearly defined.

    (d) Adequate resources are then allocated for each activity.

    (e) Work load is equally distributed to avoid stress areas and fatigue.

Organizing is thus a matter of putting together resources by matching skills with tasks, within the structural and financial constraints of an establishment. A catering manager therefore, needs to organize his staff, equipment and materials into work centres and service areas to provide optimum levels of production and service thereby giving satisfaction to staff, customers and the organization in terms of profits.

The fact that organization and therefore authority relationships between people exist in every establishment cannot be denied. Even the smallest food service has an organization structure, formally spelt out or informally created by one person instructing and others following those instructions and reporting back.

Directing

While planning and organizing require mental effort on the part of the manager, directing is the function that initiates actual performance of tasks and requires greater interactions between people.

This is done by: (a) Instructing; (b) Guiding; (c) Supervising; (d) Teaching; and (e) Reviewing.

Instructing—This is an important step because while a manager may have worked out a perfect plan of activities—indicating who is to do what, unless the instruction to the group actually carrying out the plan is clearly understood by them, paper plans can fail miserably. All instructions therefore, should be clearly written out in a language understood by the staff, then verbally communicated to them so that any queries arising from the staff can be clarified before the work actually starts. Then copies of written instructions should be placed on notice boards at suitable points in the kitchen and service areas. It is a good policy to prepare instructions for each activity and paste them at each work centre for ready reference.

In catering situations interaction is extremely important because people involved in kitchen and service areas are generally of different educational, cultural and religious backgrounds and communication is not as simple as it may seem to a manager. Staffs understands according to their own experience and abilities, and a very simple instruction like 'Please bring me some coffee' can mean different things to different people. To a server it would convey a cup of coffee, to the kitchen staff it may mean getting the manager some coffee beans to sample, to the storekeeper it may mean issuing a fresh tin of coffee, and so on. Where such a disparity of backgrounds and job skills occur, it is wise to pass on instructions to the person directly in charge of the kitchen, i.e. the head cook or kitchen supervisor depending on the size of the establishment or the organization structure of the kitchen. It is also more likely that instructions passed down to other staff in kitchens by the cook would be better received and accepted, because he is seen as one of them doing jobs with the rest. Besides it is much easier for people to follow a single leader who speaks their language and works alongside.

Instructions must ensure that each member understands how his work fits into the total scheme of work to be achieved at the end of the day, week, month and so on.

Guiding—The task of directing people involves guiding them in their jobs in a manner that will help them to achieve the standards of performance desired and also gradually develop themselves through their jobs.

There are a number of occasions when a worker does not want to admit that he is finding a problem in his job, for fear of being under rated by his colleagues or superiors. In such cases the managers or supervisors will not be able to guide him in time, if they wait for him to ask for guidance. The result will be habitual use of incorrect methods and poor performance. Therefore an important component of good direction is "supervision".

*Supervising—*Supervision involves 'keeping a watch' on what is going on at the production, service and other related activity levels. Clearly one must avoid standing too close to an employee or actually interfering with his job by performing it. There are many ways in which supervision can be carried out effectively:

(a) By viewing people's work positively. This means looking for things they are doing 'right' and giving 'praise" when it is due. In the process keen observations of other people's work too can bring out areas where guidance and correction may be necessary.

19

(b) Supervision is also possible through a regular round of activity areas of work centres just to say "hello" to people and find out about their welfare. Observations or curiosity shown about the way work is being done can often produce a response from which judgment of methods being followed can be made.

(c) Records of production and sales, statements of costs and profit margins can be a good guide to supervision. Areas showing variances with respect to expected results indicate that attention is needed.

In catering establishments, good supervision helps in maximizing resource use, because one is dealing with 'food' which can tempt just any person, especially if it is an expensive item and not easy to afford.

Teaching—The person responsible for motivating people to achieve goals, has got to be able to demonstrate methods of work which will relieve stress situations in the production and service centres. Catering is always associated with peaks and troughs, that is, moments when the tempo of work is very fast and under pressure and moments when there appears to be not enough to do. These are correlated with mealtimes when the influx of customers is maximum and then in between when it dies off.

Teaching people to organize work so that it can be spread evenly throughout the working day, and using quicker methods for finishing time-consuming jobs, makes work less stressful and performance better. In addition it helps to create a more relaxed environment for development of good human relations.

Reviewing—Reviewing the effect of every activity on individual and total performance is the job of every food director. There are a number of strategic points in the production cycle of food, which determine the quality of what is on the customer's plate. Reviewing activities therefore, and modifying them where necessary to conform to standards laid down, is essential for every food service, large or small.

Directing or leading people to work willingly and achieve organizational, group and individual goals depends greatly on the personality of the manager. His leadership style, experience and ability to communicate with people, to a large extent, determines the degree to which staff can take instruction, be guided, supervised motivated to achieve and develop.

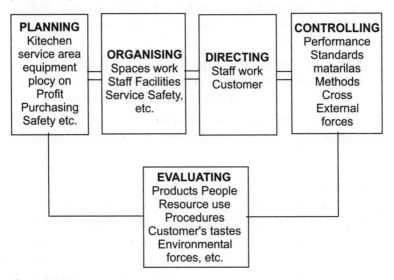

Coordinating

Besides directing individuals to achieve goals, the activities of all staff have to be well coordinated if group efforts are to become meaningful.

Henri Fayol considered coordination as the binding together, unifying and harmonizing of all activities and efforts. The larger the organization the greater becomes the extent of coordination necessary. It helps to keep the individual departments together instead of alienating their activities. Better interaction is established and work is done under a single command. Where good

21

coordination exists staff loyalty to the establishment is strengthened. A feeling of oneness permeates through the organization and results in greater understanding.

Koontz considers management as an exercise in coordination. In fact, all the functions of management need to be coordinated to achieve goals. One can imagine the chaos that can result if the purchase of food materials is not coordinated with the menus planned, or quality received is not suitable for the dish planned. Again, if service style is not linked with production and clearing operations, it can result in customer dissatisfaction and unhygienic conditions for all.

Constant coordination helps to tackle problems when they arise, gather ideas from various experiences, anticipate problems and take timely action to prevent them from recurring.

The extent of a manager's responsibility for coordination depends on the organization's structure, policies and scope of his activity.

Controlling

In all the functions of management discussed so far, there is no certainty that the targets laid down will be consistently achieved. Control is therefore necessary to give the right direction to activities. This is because achieving is no simple process-taking place under stable conditions. A changing environment consisting of helping and hindering constantly surrounds the food service establishment is constantly surrounded by a changing environment consisting of helping and hindering forces as far as achievement is concerned. Controlling the hindering forces therefore, and making use of the helping forces can achieve goals. Constant monitoring is however necessary.

The controlling function in management is expected to increase the impact of the 'helping' rather than the 'hindering' forces working in an establishment. This can only be done if managers make the best use of natural forces like a favourable crop, good weather, holiday time to attract customers, motivate staff, invest on better equipment and provide a safe, healthy and happy working environment. In such conditions people would be willing to face any challenge from the external environment. At the same time any hindering force needs to be counteracted as soon as it arises in order to ensure that activities proceed towards their original goals.

The control process has various components:

(a) Measuring actual performance.
(b) Comparing results with standards expected.
(c) Pinpointing areas of deviation.
(d) Determining reasons for the deviations.
(e) Taking corrective action, so that goals can be achieved.

Control is usually exercised through the formulation of budgets such as capital, purchase, cost, sales and operational budgets. Apart from these close supervision, regular maintenance, inspection and security measures help to establish control of operations and ensure efficient resource use.

Controlling is a very specialized but multifaceted function involving control of costs, methods of work and processes, behaviour of people at work, both individual as well as in groups, all of which have been dealt with in the units that follow.

Evaluating

How well people perform their functions can only be ascertained by comparing actual results with expected ones, over a period of time. The process of therefore judges efficiency reviewing or evaluating, which is a measure of how far set goals have been achieved. This may be done periodically by the manager himself or by his superior. A process of self-judgment or evaluation as one move towards set goals helps to ensure success. If evaluation is done at the end of a project, it can only have a theoretical

23

function because correction of procedures or deviations from set norms cannot be detected in a precise manner.

In addition, the use of resources becomes inefficient if people have to search for 'what' went wrong 'where' and 'when' on the way to the goal.

The areas of evaluation in catering establishment are:

Staff Appraisal—The performance of staff needs to be evaluated from time to time in order to determine how efficiently their potential is being tapped. Appraisal not only brings to light work carelessly done, but also helps to identify training needs or guidance needed by staff. Judgments regarding efficiency of staff made on the basis of recorded information through checklists, analysis sheets, production records, sales records and profit statements, are useful for establishing future plans for staff improvement as well as for the establishment.

Staff may be appraised with the help of rating scales designed to judge:

(a) A person's knowledge and understanding of his work
(b) The quality of performance in terms of its being 'unsatisfactory' or 'outstanding'
(c) A person's compatibility, dependability, awareness regarding safety, cleanliness, etc.;
(d) A person's integrity, loyalty in terms of willing cooperation with co-workers to help achieve organizational goals and
(e) Health status.

Apart from the above it is important to evaluate personal qualities like character, reliability, presence of mind, initiative as well as social skills. Although these are difficult to evaluate objectively, some methods need to be devised because they are important to a progressive establishment. Evaluation must be done in a very unbiased manner as far as staffs are concerned, because any impression of having favoured even one person in judgment can lead to serious repercussions in staff relations. Evaluation also provides standards for placement of staff in higher positions for which they are found to have the skills.

Evaluation of staff may reveal a high rate of staff turnover, or absenteeism indicating a lapse on the part of management in terms of not being able to motivate them enough for efficient performance and interest in their work. Alternatively, those who are constantly abstaining from work may be frequently sick, in which case action is necessary to improve their health. A third cause may be over work that calls for redistribution of jobs or investment in some labour saving devices.

Appraisal of work conditions and procedures: This involves

(a) Evaluating kitchen and service area plans to see if they require redesigning or rearranging for smoother workflow and comfort.
(b) Evaluating jobs for deciding on areas requiring mechanization for speed of work, efficiency, cleanliness and safety.
(c) The degree of lighting and ventilation required in relation to particular work centres.
(d) Evaluating structures for necessary maintenance jobs.
(e) Analysing ergonomic aspects of the work environment.
(f) Evaluating methods of serving, washing and clearing to estimate the amount of breakage. A high percentage would indicate poor quality crockery or careless handling. This may call for decisions regarding increasing investments, training of staff, etc.

Food Product Evaluation—It is necessary to see that products conform to standards laid down. This is generally done by sensory and objective methods of assessment. The sensory methods involve setting up taste panels consisting of people who are highly.sensitive to slight changes in taste, flavour, odour and colour of foods. The objective methods make use of instruments to measure qualities like thickness, flow, crispness, lightness and intensity of colour of food. The nutritional quality of food can be judged through chemical estimation of the contents of various nutrients in different foods and dishes at regular intervals.

Evaluating the quality of dishes served to the customer must be a continuous process that helps to improve the product progressively. Some aids to evaluating foods are the use of score sheets for each dish a sample of which is given in Table 1.2.

Table 1.2: Score Sheet for Tandoori Chicken.

Quality Characteristic	Score Description	Score of Sample
	1	2
Colour	Burnt Discoloured	Reddish Brown
Moisture	Too moist Dry	Just right
Mouths feel	Hard Mushy	Tender but firm
Taste and Flavour	Flat Over-seasoned	Well seasoned Natural
Raw strong Flavour	well developed	
Total	Score	

Rating scales help to establish preferences of customers for a dish especially if it is a new recipe. The scale is prepared on the basis of the descriptions indicated in Table 1.3, and various samples of the same food are subjected to preference rating.

Table 1.3: Preference rating score sheet.

PRODUCT	RATING SCORE	SAMPLES	DATE:
		A B C D E	
Excellent	5		
Very Good	4		
Good	3		
Fairly Good	2		
Not Good			
not Bad	1		
Don't Like			
very Much	0		
Dislike	0		
Total Score			
COMMENTS:			

Most food establishments depend on sensory methods of food evaluation, as it is very expensive to set up food testing laboratories and spend time on objective testing. As far as evaluation of foods for nutrients is concerned it is convenient for the caterer to use already available information in the form of nutritive value tables, which have been prepared after adequate laboratory estimations of different foods and periodically updated.

While evaluating food products the guidelines to be followed would be based on the acceptability of the food to those who prepare it and the customers, who consume it. It is therefore the practice in all establishments to taste the food for acceptably and check its colour and preventability before it is offered to the customer.

Evaluation for Profitability—All food service operations must be evaluated for viability. This involves estimating sales, costs and profit figures. If the food costs are too high it can be indicative of the following:

(a) Pilferage of food from stock.
(b) Prices too high.
(c) Cooking method inappropriate, giving inadequate portions.
(d) Menu planning unsuitable to cost structure of the establishment.
(e) Excessive wastage in preparation.
(f) Inadequate weighing facilities or supervision at strategic points in the production cycle.

All the above points indicate inefficient management, and can be corrected to reduce costs. This holds good even for overhead and labour costs.

Besides looking at profitability from the point of view of costs and sales figures, it is important to determine if seating capacity is sufficient for demand or needs to be extended. Another aspect, which reflects in high cost, is the amount of plate waste. Estimates may be made from figures of menu items often rejected by customers. A close look at the menu and deletion of unpopular items or those that the staffs are not skilled enough to prepare well will increase the viability of the establishment. Plate waste can also result from a change in customer tastes, and this too has to be watched.

It is obvious; therefore, the evaluation is necessary for ensuring continued efficiency, at all levels of the establishment.

All the functions of management therefore are closely interlinked and no one function operates in isolation, or in a particular order or sequence. They would be performed according to the needs of various situations, and to various extents as required.

All the functions need to be performed at all levels in an organization to achieve set goals.

Catering establishments by virtue of their varying sizes differ in the manner in which individual managers perform their functions. It is important to emphasize that management is independent of ownership, and all managers are not owners. It is only very small establishments like the roadside kiosks, tea stalls and canteens that may be managed by their owners. And, it is here that there is a need for developing professional attitudes to catering because, it is the entrepreneur whose resources and capacity to borrow at high interest rates are limited. He must therefore look at all the facets of catering with a view to generating the means for expansion or diversification. This can be done best by being scientific in approach to management rather than setting up one-off operations and working by rule of thumb.

It must also be recognized that no operation can run single-handed, and if one has to deal with people at work, and attract enough people to serve, operations must be based on sound principles and function in planned coordinated manner.

However, while the basic principles and functions can be leant or taught, the art of managing situations comes only with experience. Besides, it is acquired to different extents by each individual, depending on his or her ability to imbibe confidence, develop presence of mind and trust in others.

Also, developing the art of making decisions on behalf of other people and communicating effectively with them, using initiative and creativity as one goes along, requires social and creative skills, which come more easily to some than to others.

Two

Tools of Management

As the term indicates, *"tools* of management" refers to materials which have been developed by managers the past and used as an aid to effective management. These vary with the level of management and therefore each level uses different aids. The basic tool for any establishment is the organization chart, which was the structure of an organization in terms of how the various units or departments are linked together.

Organisation Chart

The organization structure is the outcome of putting people and jobs together and therefore represents the ire team involved in the running of the establishment at both operational and management levels. The chart indicates activity-authority relationships that exist in the establishment. According to Drucker, organisation structure can be charted out by using three types of analysis.

An organization chart tells us about the subordinate-superior relationships and the lines of decision making authority that exist in an establishment, in other words 'who' reports to 'whom'.

Organisation Chart

Activity Analysis	Decision Analysis	Relations Analysis
Determining activities Listing according to importance Grouping interrelated unitary ones together	Determining how far in the future, a decision will show its effect. Impact of decision functions Dependence on ethics How often decisions are taken	Defining manager's role in relation to his to goals his contribution to goals interaction with other people

It also establishes existence of unitary or dual command as the case may be, helping to correct any inconsistencies that show up on the chart. Any organization that has a detailed organization chart can be associated with set structure, having functions logically arranged to achieve maximum efficiency. These formal arrangements are based on formal leadership and methods of communication, with the hope of achieving proper coordination, because people tend to accept their positions in the organization as charted out. The two types of authority relationships that most often exist in food services are line and line-staff relationships. In the former, each individual is responsible to the person ranking above him on the organizational chart. Thus, authority and responsibility are passed downward. In the latter, that is line and staff pattern, specialists are positioned at various levels to advise those along the line structure because the activities of the establishment become too diversified for proper functioning and control. The expertise of staff is utilized to maximize the efficiency of line personnel to the utmost. However, a number of problems can arise if the information channels in an establishment strictly follow the lines of authority. In catering particularly, where staffs are expected to fill in for others at short notice, specialist departments can prove futile if informal channels of communication do not develop.

Organization structures can grow in two directions, vertically and horizontally. In vertical structured organizations the person above assigns the work to his immediate subordinates down the line. Figure indicates a vertically structured food service establishment.

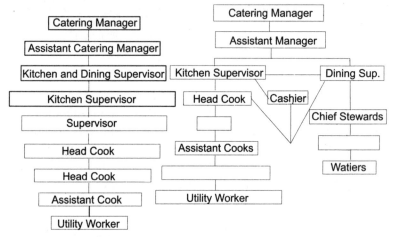

As the length of the structure increases, coordinating the activities of the establishment become difficult, so the duties get divided separately for each unit.

For example, if the control and decision-making function lies solely at the top level it is completely centralized, which means all decisions must come from the highest level. Structures may also be flat or tall which indicate the span of control at each level of the establishment. Tall structures have a shorter span of control, that is, each supervisor or manager has less number of people under his authority, than in a flat structure. In flat structures therefore it is more difficult to supervise closely.

While an organization chart can be used as a tool for managing, it also has some limitations, which are enumerated below:

(a) The charting only shows formal authority relationships,

omitting the many informal ones that develop at work and become a powerful means of communication between people. This is because these develop spontaneously between people at work, and leaders emerge within groups not because of their position but because they possess some personal qualities like age, competence charisma and behavioural patterns that command respect.

(b) The chart also does not tell us how much authority is vested in each position.

(c) Many charts indicate structures as they are expected to be, even though they may not be so in reality. A chart therefore, does not necessarily indicate an efficient, organisation of work in an establishment.

(d) The structure does not indicate the nature of management activity taking place at each level, whether operational, creative or administrative.

(e) The major disadvantage is that people begin to interpret authority relationships as differences in status.

Sometimes lines of authority are drawn at a lower level on the chart in some units than in others, or because a particular person reports to someone higher up in the organisation, his status may be confused. Some organizational charts for catering establishments of different sizes.

It will be noticed that in a 'dhaba', the relationships between manager and other staff are flexible, being both formal and informal, as is expected where staff numbers are limited and everyone on a personal level tackles all jobs. It is worth mentioning here that the 'dhaba' or roadside cafe in India is a very popular eating place and traditionally prepares food from raw ingredients and serves them to travellers piping hot, giving at the same time a very personalized service, by preparing chappatis in the form requested by customers.

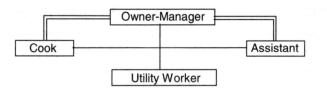

While formal relationships do not exist between the service staff and kitchen personnel, informal relationships get established if pleasant relations are harboured by managers who can then use these channels to advantage for greater efficiency.

The position description however, provides a standard against which to judge if a position is at necessary, and what its organizational level and location in the structure should be. As the organization grows larger more and more levels of authority are formed and work gets decentralized, as also its control.

Within the structures of different organizations illustrated, other tools required by a food service manager for efficient management are job description, job specification, work and time schedule, job analysis, production and service analysis statements and budgets according to the various levels in an establishment.

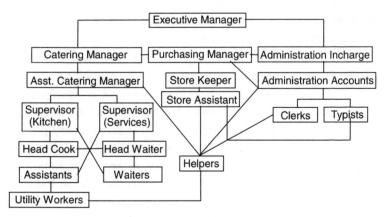

Job Description

Job description refers to the definition of a job in a precise manner indicating exactly what is to be done y people who are occupying or would be occupying a job position in an establishment. A well-defined job brings about greater certainty of what is expected in terms of the performance match expected ones; both morale and efficiency are raised. However, a job should not be too narrowly defined, as it leaves no scope for using initiative and creativity. On the other hand, too vague a description also makes it difficult to understand and handle the job, leading to frustration and loss of control.

Job descriptions are therefore effective tools for managing at every level of the organization structure. As one proceeds along the chain of command towards the operative level in the organization, job descriptions need to be more detailed, clear-cut and expressed in a language and form which can be understood by less educated workers. At higher levels people have a better knowledge of the work for which they are appointed and are expected to have a higher mental calibre. Besides, the results of their work are not immediately seen as in the case of operative staff. As the proportion of mental work increases, they have greater flexibility in timing their work, and can adjust their schedules so long as they go on feeding the information required by operating staff at the right time.

ORGANISATION LEVEL	TOOLS USED	RESPONSIBILITY
Kitchen production and service	Job description, job specification, time and work schedules. Staff duty listed/records menus	Responsible for actually producing and serving food sheets
Line management	Job analysis sheets production plans staff rotas sales analysis records	Overall supervision of production plans, requisioning of ingredients and issue from stores, directing Coordinating

(Contd.)

35

(Contd.)

ORGANISATION LEVEL	TOOLS USED	RESPONSIBILITY
Middle Management	Plans for staffing menus, absenteeism records, price lists inventory records, order sheets, standard costing sheets, budget statements, etc	Controlling preparing staff duty lists, staff requirements, ordering food and materials planning profitable menus, arranging for parties, preparing budgets, (operating) etc.
Top Management	Plans for sales, purchases, recruitment expansion, etc., decision-making communication, leadership	Setting goals, policy making for for manpower planning introducing tech. planning for profits diversification, etc.

Tools of Management Used at Different Levels of a Catering Establishment

This can be seen when we look at the job of the head cook vis-à-vis that of a catering manager's. While a chef has to report on duty at 8 a.m. to complete his various jobs and supervise those of his team in the kitchen for lunch service, the manager can work on a more flexible schedule so long as the menus are planned in advance, food materials ordered in time and meals checked for quality before they are served to customers.

It is also important to note that better communication through job descriptions is necessary whenever one is dealing with a group of people having diverse capabilities. As one goes up the organizational ladder job descriptions become more broad-based, stating only the functional aspect of the job. It need not necessarily spell out the manner (through clear-cut steps) in which the function is to be performed or goal achieved because the communication is a one to one communication with the superior, and the worker can always clarify any point verbally with his superior.

It will be noticed that the job description of a cook is more comprehensive. It also acts as a checklist for staff that may forget to do a job till it becomes routine for them. On the other hand, the job description of the catering manager is more general, expecting him to work to an efficiency guided by his experience. He is, however, given an idea of what is expected of him in terms of arranging functions, bar service and meals for staff.

Title Kitchen Supervisor Code No. Establishment

Job Summary

The job carries with it the responsibilities for:

(a) Efficient operation of catering facilities for management staff and employees.
(b) Arrangement of functions as required.
(c) Administration of bar facilities.
(d) Liasing with related departments.
(e) Holding additional charge in the absence of the superior.

Performance Requirement

(a) Responsibilities as above.
(b) Using initiative in the development of menus and methods of work.
(c) Developing good working relations with staff and guests, suppliers and visitors.
(d) Evaluating work and staff performance, and ensuring maximum utilization of resources.
(e) Ensuring optimum equipment use and maintenance.

Supervision

(a) Supervision of all production and service area work.
(b) Checking for quality.

(c) Close check on service at peak hours to look for problems such as queuing, delay in service and feedback customers.

(d) Getting feedback from customers.

Job description of a catering supervisor.

Title Head Chef Code Number Establishment

Job Summary

The job involves:

(a) Planning menus with catering supervisor.
(b) Requisitioning ingredients for food preparation.
(c) Checking deliveries with requisition slips.
(d) Checking quality of food received and getting it issued for use or storage in kitchen as required.
(e) Allotting work to assistant cooks.
(f) Guiding them in preparation and processing techniques.
(g) Preparing main dishes.
(h) Finishing all food.
(i) Testing for acceptability.
(j) Dishing out, portioning and holding food at the right temperatures till required for service.
(k) Getting next day's menus checked, requisitioning ingredients and sending requests to stores for issue.
(l) Getting preparations done and refrigerated for use next morning.
(m) Getting kitchen cleared up at the end of each day, switching off gas, electricity and water points.
(n) Locking up, or handing over work to the person taking over for the next shift as the case may be.

Job Description of a Head Cook

It can therefore be generalized, that job descriptions are not only important aids to job performance at all levels of an organization but they help to draw up recruitment requirements, set up salary levels commensurate with work involved, provide the guidelines for training and aid in controlling activities within the establishment. Job descriptions also remove conflicts between people in terms of specifying each person's job responsibilities.

Job Specification

A job specification is a statement indicating standards to be achieved for a particular job. It also covers duties expected to be performed, working conditions in which the job would be carried out, and the qualifications required. A job specification is generally used as a tool for selection of the right employee for a particular job. Small establishments may use the job description instead of the job specification for the purpose, because closer supervision is possible at work, to check if expected standards of performance are achieved at every stage of production as service. A sample job specification is given below.

Job Title:	**Cook**
Department:	Kitchen.
Supervisor:	Catering Manager.
Job summary:	As under job description.
Education:	Craft course in catering.
Experience required:	At least two years experience in an institutional kitchen.
Knowledge and skills:	Knowledge of Indian and continental cooking.
Personal standards:	Clean appearance and habits.
References required:	One at work and one personal.
Hours of work:	40 hours a week.
Promotional opportunities:	To head cook, and with extra qualification to kitchen supervisor.

Ability tests: Actual performance tests to be passed to expected standards.

A Sanple Job Specification

Work Schedule

This represents an outline of the work to be done by an employee. When this is to be completed within a time schedule as well, then it is referred to as a time and activity plan.

For proper scheduling it is important to analyse tasks that are to be performed on a particular day. In catering, the production day can be divided into low and high production periods, and an understanding of these is important in scheduling task. As a rule tasks requiring minimum effort, time and attention, should be scheduled or planned for performance during periods of low production, as these follow high-pressure work periods of peak-hour production and service. Besides providing the necessary relaxation, such scheduling gives a sense of achievement and motivates staff to cope with the pressures of peak hours. On the other hand, if complicated tasks are fixed for a low production period, they appear to get more complicated.

The best time to schedule such tasks is first thing in the morning when workers are fresh and rested. However, sometimes-catering staffs are required to work late hours, and perhaps continue in the morning because of the high rate of staff absenteeism or turnover. In such cases people who have worked more than eight hours a day should be given simple jobs, which do not require a lot of care and attention, because mental and physical fatigue sets in.

A job considered disagreeable by a worker should only be scheduled during peak hours when it gets done in the stride because people do not have the time to think of it in particular. If all jobs are considered in the light of their physical, psychological, social and environmental effects on the performers, work a number of advantage:

(a) More work can be done in a day, imparting a sense of achievement.
(b) Resources are better utilized, making work more productive.
(c) A busy schedule leaves very little idle time, gives greater satisfaction, and raises staff morale.
(d) The involvement is greater and staffs perform their best.

Apart from work and time scheduling, productive work depends a lot on people's attitudes to their the nature of the job, the time and concentration required to perform it and the amount of satisfaction derived from it. Analysing tasks and scheduling work can therefore help to identify materials, equipment time and skills, required for doing particular jobs. It is an effective tool for efficient working, as it helps to establish a sequence in which jobs are to be done within a time frame. This sequence is readily available before the work is started, so it helps each worker to know what he has to do, without waiting for verbal instructions and wasting time. Above is a sample work schedule for a self-service canteen operating between 10 a.m. and 5 p.m., offering a choice of plated lunches, snacks sweets and beverages. It will be noticed that at the peak hours of production and service, that is 10.00 a.m. to 2.00p.m. all the staff are present. The peak period lies between 10.30 a.m. and 12.00 noon for production and 12.30 p.m. and 1.30 p.m. for service. The timings for staff are therefore staggered before and after the peak hours.

Work and time schedules not only chalk out the work plan for staff, but at a glance help to identify tasks which may be combined, eliminated, or modified for greater efficiency. For effective scheduling a catering manager must have data on the time required for performing a particular job.

Schedules are important tools for demarcating the responsibilities of each worker and giving them a sense of achievement at the end of a task. A schedule may also indicate changes or additions to normal duties on a particular day, and helps to check any claims for overtime work performed. Often greater use of convenience foods on the menu or introduction of time and labour saving equipment may require time and task adjustments on the schedule. Flexibility should always be built into schedules, to enable food services to adjust their work in response to technological and other environmental changes.

The food industry is unique in the sense that there is a constant need to increase or decrease staff strength at the production and service levels, depending on the number of customers and their requirements. It is also a common feature of the industry to employee low paid workers and therefore, on a particular day, there may be even 10 to 20 per cent absenteeism. To guard against such circumstances, the work force consists of casual workers on hourly or daily work basis, temporary employees, ad hoc appointees, those on training and so on. This enables a manager to use scheduling as a tool to cover peak hour work adequately by the required number of people, without resistance from staff. In catering, split shift schedules are rarely followed, though staff may be asked to perform day or night duties through alternate weeks if an establishment does operate round the clock. This, however, is not normally done in any food service, because people do not generally eat round the clock. Besides, laws governing food service establishments spell out the desired hours of work in accordance with minimum wage agreements for various types of work.

Work and staff need to be scheduled properly for two main reasons:

(a) *To have the right type of skills available when required:* for instance, there is need to have more service staff available at lunch time in a food service establishment, rather than kitchen staff. Once the food is ready only one or two back-up staff in the kitchen are necessary for ensuring a constant flow of food from kitchen to service counter. The number will of course depend on the type of the service and the customer.

(b) *For maximum efficiency:* This is possible only if production and service areas are not overcrowded, or else the work environment will not only cause fatigue but also become prone to accidents. Successful scheduling in terms of man-hours and skills can only be done if jobs are analysed properly along with working conditions, menu patterns, purchasing methods, quantities handled and equipment required.

Job Analysis

The term clearly means analysing jobs to know precisely what they involve. The purpose of breaking up jobs into their respective components is to take an objective look at a job at frequent intervals. This helps to bring into focus any overlapping, neglected or problem areas, which can then be remedied by conscious effort, to increase efficiency. Job analysis is also sometimes referred to as 'task analysis' and is a way of looking at jobs and situations in which a number of variables are involved.

Catering situations are made up of a number of interdependent parts of variables, and job analysis helps to simplify them and reveal possibilities for improvement. This is more so in the changing technological environment of today, in which the possibilities of making labour intensive jobs easier and less time-consuming are enormous.

Jobs may be analysed by many methods, such as charting out the steps or a performer and preparing travel patterns for a job.

These records are known as 'pathway charts' and help to analyse areas where unnecessary time and energy is being used. The data can then be used to develop procedures and aids for better resource use.

Task analysis also helps in scheduling work, by examining it closely for process, materials, equipment and skills, etc. needed to complete a job. A figure below shows the steps or activities involved in preparing a sandwich.

An examination of the steps will indicate whether,

(a) Some of them can be combined into a single step,
(b) The sequence is interrupted or logical for a smooth work flow, and
(c) Time and energy spent can be reduced through scheduling

Task analysis for sandwich preparation

STEP	ACTIVITY
1.	Collecting ingredients together.
2.	Buttering the slices.
3.	Preparing the filling.
4.	Spreading filling between slices and pressing them together.
5.	Wrapping in damp cloth, and keeping refrigerated till required for service.
6.	Removing from refrigerator and trimming sides.
7.	Cutting and shaping the sandwiches.
8.	Arranging in service plate or packing in portions as required and sending for service.

Some tasks may be coupled or performed simultaneously. For instance, activity (2) and (3) may be combined to eliminate the step of buttering the slices. Mixing the butter in the ingredients of the filling can do this.

Job analysis is therefore a very good tool for increasing efficiency both in terms of speed as well as resource utilization and can be used at all levels of activity, more so at the operational level. Job analysis sheets help to assess the skills required for each task and formulate job descriptions, which usually define duties, tasks and responsibilities of the performer.

Production Service and Staff Analysis Statements

Statements indicating the quantities or portions of food produced, served and left over each day act as tools for forecasting customer demand patterns over a particular period of time. The types of records are production records, sales charts, records of stocks and leftovers over a specified period menu records and standard costing sheets. A catering manager according to the specific requirements of the establishment can develop any number of tools. Standard costing sheets, for instance, help in substituting equally costed dishes when some ingredients for a planned dish on the menu are not available or have become too costly for the dish to be profitably produced and offered to the customer.

Each establishment can thus devise certain records, which are suitable for controlling and managing its operation. Another aid is a record of staff absenteeism. This can help to analyse which workers are constantly absenting them from work. The reason could well be traced to routine ness of the job, insecurity at work or ill health. These reasons if identified can lead management to take corrective action. Records of sickness and absenteeism also indicate productive hours lost, leading to increasing labour costs which catering managers can least afford?

Budget

A budget is a projected plan for the operation of a business. It is sometimes expressed in terms of money, but at other times may also be expressed in units or as percentages. It is an important tool for managing an operation as it establishes targets for future production, sales, staff numbers, purchases and so on.

Budgets are of different kinds and are classified according to the use for which they are intended and designed in various establishments.

Figure below shows the kinds of budgets that may be formulated by catering establishments depending on their size.

Budgets may also be referred to as fixed or flexible with respect to the levels of sales assumed. In fixed budgets, the amount to be spent on certain items is fixed at the beginning of a budget period. In flexible ones, a judgment of costs is made from previous years experiences in relation to the possible volume of sales. Food services that are subject to seasonal sales like canteens and cafeterias situated in hill resorts or at sea sides also prepare flexible budgets for labour costs.

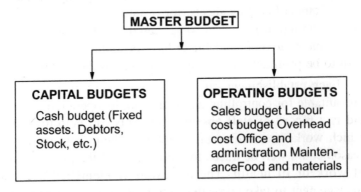

Kinds of Budgets in Catering Establishments

Budgets are prepared on basis of forecasts of sales volume, which in turn help to determine:

   (i)   The proportion of variable and semi-variable costs;

  (ii)   The cash position of the establishment; and

 (iii)   The amount of expenditure to be made on equipment, furniture and overheads,

In every establishment, however, there are certain key factors that govern the volume of sales achieved, and these need to be considered metimes known as "limiting factors". Some of these factors are:

(i) *Capital at hand:* It is not possible to invest more than a certain amount, and this factor limits the extent to which an establishment can grow.

(ii) *Size of spaces:* This affects the seating capacity. It is obvious that more customers cannot be served at a time than the space available permits.

(iii) *Staff at hand:* Shortage of staff limits the production and sale of food and services to the capacity of existing staff. Being short staffed therefore is a limiting factor for sales volume of an establishment.

(iv) *Poor management:* In spite of having enough resources their poor management can become a serious limitation to achieving profits. Standards deteriorate through poorly planned menus, improper work distribution, inefficient kitchen arrangements, poor supervision, inaccurate costing and pricing.

(v) *Demand of the customer:* The demand for food may decrease because of high prices, greater competition or an epidemic because of which people abstain from eating out. It is therefore important to identify which factor is limiting the sales in a particular situation and then try to remove its effect on the establishment.

The managers of small establishments are particularly concerned with operating budgets, such as sales, labour, overhead, maintenance and administrative budgets. In larger establishments at higher levels in an organization the cash and capital budgets become important tools for setting goals, controlling and monitoring performance and quality of food and service. Along with budgets accounting information through balance sheets, profit and loss accounts and break-even charts, all act as tools for effective management of operations.

The tools of management discussed so far were all concrete and expressible on paper. Those that follow are subtler in nature, but are nevertheless indispensable for making them bring out their help for the organisation.

Leadership Style

The leadership role of a manager concerns his personal relationships with ... subordinates ... how much he can communicate with them. Leadership is the quality of a manager, irrespective of his rank and position that directly influences people's behaviour towards work and their work. In other words, it is the quality by which people can be motivated to move enthusiastically and with confidence towards established goals. Leadership qualities are inborn to a certain extent, but can also be acquired by training and experience. Leadership styles adopted in the management of group work are closely related to the personality of individual managers and their social skills. It is debatable, how far social skills can be taught, because extrovert personalities develop easy relations with other people while introverts find it more difficult.

The different leadership styles that are used in the catering field can be easily classified. Some distinctly make people work by order or force, others join the group and initiate activity, still others use persuasion while some, by their pleasant and endearing manner generate the enthusiasm for work and achieve goals in the best possible manner. Thus, through a manager's personality, referred to by Doswell and Gamble as the 'manager factor', a manager can build an image for himself in his work environment. For the establishment he is responsible for how customers view the food service.

Katz and Kahn define leadership as "the influential increment over and above mechanical compliance with the routine directives of the organization."

It is the willingness of people to follow a leader, and this happens when people can see the manager or leader as one who is providing their own wants and needs.

Leadership style is used as an effective tool of management both in formal as well as informal structures. This is evident from the fact that even when placed formally in positions of power,

Managers can exercise authority over people only if they will accept it. Some managers who are good planners and organizers fail to achieve results because they are not good leaders. Reference has already been made to the development of informal organization patterns within the formal framework.

In catering situations one often sees the emergence of a leader within a group, that is, a person who will be followed in whatever he says or does, even though he may not have been placed in a position of authority through the formal structure.

Experiences of managers have shown that the contribution of leadership ability towards goal achievement may extend up to 40 per cent while 60 per cent is attributed to the need for the job and the authority exercised by superiors.

Lal has reported that managers tend to behave in characteristic ways while making decisions. Table below summarizes the style of leadership researched and the conclusions drawn.

Thus a manager does not and cannot use any one leadership style in isolation at all times. He may be autocratic in an emergency like when an accident takes place or a fire breaks out in the kitchen. Also, in situations where only he has the answer, such as deciding on the number of customers to be catered for.

According to Likert, effective managers use the participative style and depend more on communication, while at the same time adopting a supportive attitude, sharing their needs, values, goals and expectations with their staff. Various traits related to leadership ability have been identified in the literature ranging from physical traits to those of intelligence, ability, personality, social and task related ones.

Table 2.1: Styles of Leadership Prevailing among Managers

Style	Description
Own decision without explanation to subordinate.	Autocratic or centralised
Own decision with explanation to subordinate	Same as I.
Prior consolation with subordinate	Participative or decentralised
Joint decision,	Democratic
Delegation	Lassez faire

All the styles are used to different extents by managers according to the nature of the decision to be made. For example, for decisions regarding salary, styles (i) and (ii) were used 98.44 per cent of the time. For hiring staff these were used only 14 per cent of the time. The observations from this study were averaged to show the percentage of time which managers spent using the different styles of leadership.

Leadership Styles

Indicates varied percentage usages, depending on the nature and type of establishment.

Leadership style is thus a powerful tool of management, especially in people oriented spheres such catering, in which the degree of concern managers have for people (reflected in their style) can create a comfortable working environment harbouring trust and respect for each other. This of course is based entirely on the personality and other traits of the manager and his ability to inspire confidence in people, who then get committed to the goals of the establishment.

Training

With catering becoming more and more competitive, professional training of employees at all levels is becoming an indispensable tool for the management of catering operations. This is because training imparts knowledge of the various aspects of the operation, and skills to deal with the influences of the ever-changing environment. Besides ensuring efficiency training also develops the right attitudes to work. With the increasing number of unemployed graduates in the market, caterers would do well to pick up raw hands and spend less on interviews, references and selection, and subject them to on-the-job training, using training as the tool for developing their best potential. They could be subjected to on-the-job training for 70 per cent of the time, with the remaining 30 per cent utilised for academic work.

Sensitivity training should form part of the programme in which people are brought together in groups and allowed to discuss their feelings and frustrations, freely among themselves. These are referred to as T-groups. Through such exposure individuals develop trust in them and in others, become, fearless and self-confident and learn to work effectively with other people.

When people are trained in groups, they get better stimulated to learn because of group participation, and this group spirit is later maintained at work. Training programmes conducted by well-trained teachers should impart knowledge of the history and objectives of the establishment, relationships with other departments, the key persons to contact in each department, budget estimates as they affect the workers, preparation and service of food, sanitation and safety, and the existence of work improvement programmes. In addition, knowledge about laws governing food service organizations and their implications at work are a vital aspect of any training in catering.

The organization gains from a well-trained work force through reduction of staff turnover and absenteeism, fewer accidents at work, better resource utilization, decreased costs, higher production, higher levels of morale and job satisfaction. Training makes its contribution to the goals of the establishment as well as to the development of the individuals.

Decision-Making

No work at any level can be performed without making decisions. The difference lies only in the nature of the decision. At kitchen and service levels the decisions made concern materials, methods of work, quantities and quality. Higher up in the organisation decisions change to those of planning menus, selecting equipment and suppliers, making purchases, costing and pricing. Still further up the management hierarchy decisions regarding staffing, grievance procedures, trade union negotiations, establishment policies and investment have to be taken. Besides these, strategies for reacting to environmental changes have to be drawn out.

The process of decision-making involves three basic steps:

(a) Making a mental effort,
(b) Listing out alternative courses of action within the structure of a situation,
(c) Choosing a single course of action from among many alternatives.

In practice, people are making decisions all the time, without thinking about the process that the mind is going through, to decide what is to be done. For example, a cook decides to garnish a dish of tandoori chicken with onions, lemon slices and chopped coriander for one set of customers, to others he sends it accompanied by roast potatoes garnished with coriander sauce. He may have decided to do the latter because there were some boiled potatoes left over from the earlier meal or the coriander was not looking too fresh to be used as such for the last lot of customers. In both cases however, he has acted on a single course of action without as much as sitting down to list the alternatives. Similarly, the catering manager decides to change the menu because the price of a food item has suddenly gone up or down, or because he envisages a drop in the number of customers on a particular day. In this way there are so many decisions, all of different types that are being made and acted upon at all levels of management, almost continuously, depending on the roles that people are performing at work. The more complicated the decision situation, the more time is spent on decision-making.

Three pre-requisites are therefore essential for any decision to be made:

(i)   There has to be a reason for making a decision,
(ii) The courses of action that are open need to satisfy the reason, and
(iii) Choice has to be made from among these courses.

The proportions of time spent on each of the phases of decision-making vary from one level in the organization to another, and from one person to another. But, in general, at top management levels more time is spent on studying the effects of environmental changes on the establishment and developing courses of action to react to them favourably. The middle level managers spend more time selecting the best courses of action open to them.

There are two main types of decisions taken in catering establishments. Some are routine and repetitive which do not require fresh thinking each time the need arises. An example of this type is, the decision to place a pan on the cooking range when any food is to be cooked, or switching on the oven when a cake mixture is being prepared. Such decisions are said to be programmed. The second type are decisions which are unprogrammed these include those required to be taken if an accident takes place in the kitchen, or when some incident of misbehaviour has to be tackled, or a piece of equipment breaks down in the middle of food being cooked in it, or 25 per cent staff do not turn up for work one morning. These types of decisions require the use of judgment, creativity, presence of mind and initiative.

The routine type of decisions act as a tool for managing time well, because they become quite automatic and require practically no mental effort, time or advice from superiors. The unprogrammed decisions are important for managing emergency or pressure situations, which are a characteristic feature of catering establishments. At higher levels managers also need to know the possible effects of their decisions, because of the fact that catering operations consist of highly cohesive groups at the operational levels, and can collectively demonstrate group feelings bringing great pressure on management. This is expected to increase, as catering workers get more and more unionised. Decision-making, therefore, though an important tool of management needs to be used with great care, because the results of a decision are known only after a period of time. Managers would do well to cash on their knowledge of the people who work with them and utilize their cohesiveness to achieve group and organizational goals.

The importances of decisions vary with the degrees of responsibility entrusted to a manager. Where a decision has a greater effect on people, its importance is greater than a decision that affects a piece of equipment, or a procedure.

All good decisions are cost effective, and satisfying to people and the establishment. Decision-making is vital to all functions of management as it forms the core of planning. Therefore its usefulness need not be overemphasized.

Communication

All plans chalked out for the success of an establishment will come to naught, if they cannot be interpreted and understood by the people who have to carry them out. The ability to convey information or messages to others so that they can understand and interpret them in the same light, as the sender of the message is known as communication.

Communication is therefore the most important tool of management when dealing with people, yet it is the most difficult to achieve effectively, because it involves much more than just sending and receiving messages. Interpretation of what is said is affected by a number of factors such as:

(i)   Personality characteristics.
(ii)   Sense of security or fear in the work environment.
(iii)   Nationality and cultural background.
(iv)   Sex, education and occupation.

Effective tool for passing accurate information to people instead of the usual rumours. This is possible if they can identify those persons who are looked up to and trusted by the group and have liaison and leadership qualities. This cannot however, be largely depended upon as a regular means of communication, and any barriers in the way of people's understanding should be identified and removed.

Barriers to Communication

A number of factors may become barriers to effective communication and make conversation negotiation and training impossible, because people become alienated and indifferent to others and their work. These factors need to be identified constantly and guarded against to prevent communication from breaking down.

Managers have therefore got to be vigilant and maintain good human relations at all costs if an organization is to survive.

A breakdown in communication is symptomatic of the

existence of problems in the management of the organization. For example, communications can break-down if the work force is uncertain about who is the boss, how, what and when a job has to be done, or when there are no clear cut standards for staff to work towards. The uncertainty builds into confusion and frustration leading to less and less interaction between people at work. The result is inefficiency because of a demotivated workforce who does not know the goals of the establishment. If these gaps are allowed to widen communication breaks down completely. Besides the structural and organizational problems mentioned above, the reasons for communication gaps might be connected with the manner in which messages are transmitted to the people at work.

The establishment of an effective communication system in many organizations is thus the solution to a lot of deep-rooted problems, which can be brought to the surface and tackled successfully by every enterprising manager. Every manager should endeavour to identify the existing barriers to communication in the establishment, and make a conscious effort to demolish them, replacing the barriers with strings of understanding, confidence and strength.

In conclusion, tools to a manager are as useful as he can make them. If he has initiative, and the will to succeed, he can create new tools or shape old ones to suit his particular needs.

Three

Management of Resources

Introduction

Resources are factors available to a catering manager for the production and service of food, and these are always limited for a number of reasons. Some are used up and finished with time, so they have to be continually generated to have a constant supply. Others gradually wear out or depreciate in value and utility and need to be constantly maintained till unfit for use, and replaced when they become absolute.

Space or land is perhaps the only resource that in real terms appreciates with time. This appreciation, however, is only beneficial if the owner of the food service receives the advantage. In small catering establishments however, more often than not, the owner may be paying a rent for the space, in which case he does not receive the advantage of its appreciation. On the contrary, over a period of time more money is required to pay for increased rent, cutting into the profitability of the food service operation.

It is therefore evident, that for an establishment to survive in its ever-changing and competitive environment, resources need to be utilized to their maximum, because no resource can be increased indefinitely. The discussion that follows focuses attention on the utility of each resource available to a food service manager. It will be noticed that while eight kinds of resources have been identified in they cannot by their mere presence lead to the success of a food service. Resources need to be nurtured and skilfully utilized through imaginative and innovative management techniques, to make them grow and bear fruit. This has become necessary because, the environment is changing all the time, requiring managers to continually keep pace with the new challenges. Therefore the most important resources for any establishment today is its 'management skill.' When this resource is well developed, all others can be utilized to advantage. Each resource has been briefly discussed below.

Money

The goal of every food service establishment is to make profits, but before it can achieve this goal there has to be money to invest and spend in order to acquire the other resources necessary for the production and service of food. It is only when food is available to, the customer that money will start flowing back into the establishment. It would therefore be appropriate to pinpoint briefly the methods by which an entrepreneur can raise the money for his establishment, before the utilization aspect is considered. Some methods of raising money are:

(a) Borrowing from nationalized banks or government finance companies. In the case of institutions serving social causes such as catering for handicapped homes, or providing employment opportunities for war widows through setting up canteens, capital may be raised at low interest rates. Money can also be borrowed against securities or overdrafts.

(b) Joining in partnership with other people who can share the investment in the business.

(c) Purchase premises and equipment on a hire purchase basis, which can then be paid for in instalments, after the establishment is in operation.

(d) The owner can use his savings initially, till the establishment earns enough profit to pay back. But this is not a desirable practice if loans can be raised at reasonable interest rates.

Having raised the money it is important to pay it back at the earliest to minimize interest payments. In order to do this it must be invested wisely in space, equipment, materials and other resources, to get optimum return on investment. Making investment decisions for catering establishments therefore, must be based on certain general criteria such as:

(i) *Area of the space within the building:* This should be adequate to cope with the expected number of customers, and the range of services to be offered in the short as well as the long run.

(ii) *Suitability:* Each planned area in terms of design of equipment, furniture, fittings, structure, surfaces, etc. should be ergonomically suitable for use by staff and customers. At the same time it should provide an efficient, comfortable and safe working and dining environment. It is at the layout and design stage that maximum utilisation of areas need to be considered, in the light of predetermined objectives.

(iii) *Control system:* Each part of the premises must provide the means for a built-in control system. In the case of food services, it amounts to watching relevant areas and instituting methods of control at receiving, production, service and storage points. This includes attention to equipment in terms of the space available and its safety in operation.

59

(iv) *Economy in operation:* Control of operating and maintenance costs is important in all areas and for all equipment installed. Reducing man-hours required for operation by installing devices for routine jobs can minimize these costs. The concept of multiuse areas and equipment in food services is important to utilize money spent on premises wisely,

(v) *Flexibility:* If installations and spaces are designed for flexibility, smaller are as are required for a number of different activities. In addition, less equipment needs to be purchased if they are multiuse pieces.

(vi) *Durability:* The durability of materials and equipment naturally makes the money go further than if replacements are necessary early.

(vii) *Continuity:* This implies continuity in the use of areas, equipment and materials within an establishment. Any under utilization of these resources amounts to wastage.

(viii) *Efficiency:* This can be judged on the basis of how quickly after the investment is made, can the establishment pay it back with interest which has accrued.

(ix) *Safety:* This is a prime consideration when making investment decisions, and investing borrowed money.

Practically all these criteria have been discussed under separate units dealing with areas, equipment, financial aspects and safety. However, a constant review or evaluation is necessary to ensure that investments made in food service are producing the expected returns. This is because the success of catering operations depends to a large extent on the customers, and a changing environment. Once the profit areas are identified more money can be spent on them and withdraw from less profitable areas.

Space

Space being the most expensive resource requires thought for building upon it. The aim should be to utilize every square centimetre effectively. Spaces for food services may be acquired through auction, hire purchase methods, direct purchase of land or building, as considered suitable. In an existing building, spaces may be renovated to provide arrangements of work areas with equipment so placed as to establish a smooth workflow. The environment should also be congenial and comfortable to work in.

Materials

The materials commonly used in a catering establishment are food materials, table linen appointments, kitchen cloths and cleaning materials.

Food Materials

These vary from perishable fruits and vegetables, milk and meat to longer lasting grains, pulses and water. In addition, a wide variety of processed, packaged foods may be used depending on the nature of the establishment, the menu, and establishment policy concerning cooking, serving and buying methods. When purchasing food materials the points to consider for maximum utility are:

(a) Buy seasonal foods as they are cheapest in season and also contain maximum flavour, colour and nutrients.
(b) Consider percentage of edible portion when buying.
(c) Match quality, variety and the pack of food material to the end use for which it is purchased. For example, the more expensive long grain rice is suitable for those dishes in which the grain of the rice is visible when served and adds to the appearance of the dish. For dishes such as rice puddings or fermented products of rice like idli, and dosa, the cheaper broken rice would give equally good results. It may be argued, that the flavour of long grain rice is better, but this can also be obtained from broken

61

rice of the same aromatic variety. Again, there is no point in buying a bag of 100 kg bread flour when a canteen usually buys bread from the market, making fruit bun only occasionally.

(d) Match quantity purchased to storage area and type of storage (dry or cold). Also buy quantities in relation to the turnover of the food materials, which is its rate of usage.

(e) Relate purchase lists strictly to the menu and vice versa, especially when perishable commodities are purchased.

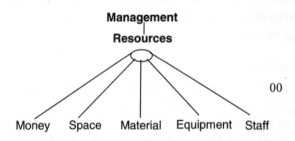

In general, food materials are best utilized when loss is prevented during receiving, storage, preparation, cooking, service and clearing. Indications of inadequate utilization are excessive plate waste, insufficient food to meet the demand, excessive leftovers, a drop in demand and soon. Any efforts to prevent these can lead to better utilization. Even water that is taken for granted needs to be used efficiently. Managers need to be in touch with the latest technology to save this resource. An electronic water tap that has no knobs or pedals is an interesting and useful device. It is controlled by an electronic photocell. Water, one has just to place hands or other objects under the tap. On removal the water flow stops) automatically. The tap is also equipped with mixers to regulate the temperature of the water. Nearly 85 per cent saving in water consumption has been reported by this device. The taps do not require any maintenance as they do not leak or drip. The taps are powered by an AC current of 220 volts

(V) and 50 Hertz (Hz) and the body is shock proof and fire-resistant.

Cleaning Materials

Cleaning materials are easily wasted especially in large establishments because they are not the focus of attention of supervisors. What is noticed is a clean kitchen, piece of equipment, a surface or a clean plate or table linen. Without doubt use of extra detergent in washing and cleaning will produce a clean effect, but so does using just enough. Excess use is not only damaging to the equipment but also to the bank balance of the establishment. Control in this area, though difficult, is essential. More attention to training people in the use of measures for detergents in terms of cups per sink of water or tablespoon per wash can lead to drastic changes in profitability.

For floor cleaning the caps of detergent containers to a bucket of water is easier for a utility worker to follow than millilitres of phenyl, for instance. Thus, practical methods of control need to be worked out for individual establishments, depending on the methods of cleaning used and the type and volume of cleaning required for utensils, crockery, cutlery, table tops and equipment.

In general, multipurpose cleaners are cheaper to buy and easier to use for a number of different surfaces and utensils, instead of a different detergent for equipment, surfaces, utensils, crockery and so on. At most, two types of detergents and one disinfectant may be used in any establishment.

Cleaning materials also include mopping buckets, mops and brooms. With a greater range being marketed everyday the prices vary a great deal, but utility and not the price should be the criteria for selection. Sometimes cheaper products clean just as well as the more expensive ones, which are priced higher because of higher overhead costs or a trade name. It is therefore wrong policy to relate price to cleaning quality. Any materials or cleaning equipment should be weighted in terms of its useful parts and not the quality of its handle or accessories. The ease of replacement of used parts and durability is also an important feature to be considered. Sometimes the simplest broom and a mop cloth may be the best choice, because they eliminate maintenance costs and time in repair, since they are discarded when worn out and replaced at very low costs, quite easily.

While cleanliness is a vital part of every activity in a food service, sophistication in cleaning equipment should be the least important unless its utility far outweighs its costs of maintenance arid storage. Small establishments with which we are mostly concerned can ill afford the facilities of cleaning firms which are now developing, and would do best to resort to buying simple, easy to use equipment. Also, utility workers employed for cleaning jobs in small establishments are generally low paid, not so literate and are untrained in so far as following written instructions or handling unfamiliar equipment is concerned. Good management demands that even the so-called common sense jobs be demonstrated to staff because they can learn better by imitation rather than through formal methods of communication. This is particularly so with methods of cleaning various types of materials, because among staff who are handling cleaning jobs, common sense is really not so common as is assumed.

The maximum utility of cleaning materials therefore, lies in establishing correct methods of cleaning, choosing simple, familiar, low cost equipment, using multipurpose detergents and avoiding wastage by buying packs in sizes required for a month or more depending on establishment needs, and finally storing well.

Table Ware

The next group of materials needed in food service is tableware such as linen and appointments. Linen includes kitchen cloths, dusters and table linen. The former are required to be sterilized by boiling for half an hour in detergent water, rinsing out the detergent and drying for reuse. Since these cloths need to be changed everyday, the most efficient way to utilize them is to distribute two dusters and a kitchen cloth to each staff member working in kitchens and serving areas, so that they are responsible for them, and use their own cloths for their work only. Replacements are then necessary only when pieces are put out of use. In larger establishments however, each day's used cloths are centrally laundered and fresh issues made each morning.

Easy clean materials or disposables however, are fast replacing use of table linen. Most cafeterias, coffee shops and even restaurants now use plastic coated tablemats, or disposable paper mats, to offset the high laundering costs of linen. In school, college and office lunchrooms tray service eliminates the need for any tablemats or linen, the tray acting as the cover for the place setting. In most food services where self-service is prevalent, paper napkins are now provided to avoid laundry expenses.

Equipment

The factors for the selection of equipment in relation to individual food service requirements have been dealt with in next chapter. These have been discussed with relevance to optimum utilization of this resource. It would suffice here to mention that equipment are expensive and if they remain unused for most of the working day in any area of use, they become uneconomic.

Another factor to be considered when investing on equipment is to ensure that its installation and utility outweigh the cost of labour that would be required to do the job if the equipment was not installed.

For maximizing use of equipment therefore, its selection must be made on the basis of:

(a) Lower labour cost.
(b) Making monotonous jobs quicker and easier.
(c) Making the environment more attractive and clean.
(d) Higher staff morale.
(e) Providing a means of adding interest to jobs and increasing the avenues for job and staff development.
(f) Increasing production capacity within the limited spaces available.
(g) Having multi uses so that the equipment does not lie idle for too long.

Every catering manager must think in terms of modular equipment, mobility to provide flexibility of arrangement and use to make investment on this resource worthwhile.

Staff

Catering establishments being service oriented are totally dependent on the skills and motivations of their staff, and their willingness to make the establishment succeed. No amount of mechanization can give that personal touch to food that the production staff can, or replace the smile so necessary to lure customers to a food service.

Staffs in food service establishments are at various levels of literacy, and possess little to highly specialized skills according to the needs of various tasks involved in food production and service. Getting the most out of people at work, and making their individual tasks and goals fit well into those of the establishment and the customer's is a difficult but challenging job for every catering manager. This is because people behave and react to situations and other people in many different ways.

Maximum utilization of staff therefore, depends on a thorough understanding of the needs of people, through establishing an effective communication system.

Maslow's need hierarchy is well established as the basis for judging what needs of individuals is satisfied at each level of the organization and what remain to be fulfilled. Further, studies of the behaviour of people at work in the 60's and 70's led to the formation of Herzberg's 'hygiene-motivation' theory which categorized factors in the environment as 'hygiene' factors, responsible for making people at work comfortable, but not motivating them enough to increase their efforts. He classed only those factors as motivators that were related to people's recognition, status and self-development and called them 'satisfiers'. It is the latter that could in Herzberg's observations increase productivity. In the 80's, however, Norman MacQueen challenged Herzberg's theory saying, "that it least applies to the people management most wants to motivate, that is, those with monotonous, repetitive, uninteresting jobs". And some jobs in catering precisely fit this description.

While Herzberg's ideas of making jobs were interesting and satisfying in order to motivate people to work better are logical, they apply only to those jobs that can be easily redesigned and enriched. If catering establishments, the work of the person washing dishes can be thought of as being enriched by the provision of dish washing machine today, but will this make him perform more or better? He will, infact, be working less and getting more idle time, perhaps even being demoralized at being gradually made redundant. There is evidence that many workers do not care whether their jobs are enriched or not, and these are usually the semi or unskilled people. Argyris believed that with time people developed apathy towards jobs and did not expect satisfaction from their work. In fact a number of studies suggest that work is done for money, while pleasures and satisfaction are sought outside the work environment as far as staff at operative levels are concerned. In such cases, to get better performance, more attention of managers would be required to provide equipment which helps to do more in less time, leaving the worker more free time to be trained for better techniques. Further, overtime payments can be reduced, leading to a lower labour cost.

Skilled staff at operative levels, such as, the head cook or chef perhaps find it already satisfying to order people around in the kitchen, show his skills in food preparation and presentation to superiors, customers and so on. Providing greater opportunities to show their skills through function catering, in addition to normal routine work can enrich their jobs further. They may also be taught skills of menu planning, maintaining kitchen records, etc. to increase their potential and usefulness.

Managers therefore need to motivate their human resources to an extent that will automatically make people perform their best. They can cash in on the fact that although the higher needs of lower level workers are satisfied mostly outside their work environment; they can still be attached to their work. Managers need therefore to ensure that the basic conditions of comfort are provided at work and an atmosphere where cordial social interaction is possible while at work or rest. The social factors affecting worker behaviour and attitudes cannot be underrated.

In catering, the two major costs when calculated as percentages of average sales are raw materials and labour. Quoting from a study these amounts to 38 and 40 per cent respectively, the remaining 22 per cent being distributed between overheads, rent and profit. Such high labour costs indicate that staff productivity is not optimised. In order to utilize people potential to the maximum, it is imperative to plan every stage of production carefully, in order to minimize idle time of staff. It stands to reason that if people receive ingredients and instructions in time, have the right equipment in working order for the job, have a comfortable working environment, and a friendly atmosphere, they are likely to do their best. This is, of course, possible only if the staff have the right skills for the job.

68

Another point that is closely linked with higher productivity and better performance is training of staff to acquire special skills needed to operate new machinery or adapt to change. According to Peter Mitchell the policy of multiskilling staff instead of making them specialists, increases performance. Apart from using up idle time from one task for doing something else, people equipped with a range of skills also help to breakdown the formal relationships created by a hierarchical organization structure. Another great advantage is that internal promotions can become the policy if greater motivation to staff is provided to improve their skills, at the same time this would reduce the high rates of labour turnover in the long run, which are known to sap the efficiency in the catering industry.

More often than not, labour turnover is accepted as a norm by some managers, in which case it is a reflection of poor staff management rather than the instability of staff, and their unwillingness to stay on the job. With more attention to the principles of organization and management therefore, staff turnover can be reduced and consequently costs and apathy too. Some methods of reducing labour turnover are:

(i)   Good pay.
(ii) Favourable conditions of work.
(iii) Demonstrating how each person's work forms a useful component of the total goal.
(iv) Participation in decisions that affect individual jobs.
(v)   Taking care of people through employee welfare schemes.
(vi) Creating a sense of belonging.

To get the best out of staff therefore, it is important to:

(a) Integrate staff goals with organizational goals.
(b) Develop good relations with people.
(c) Look for what each person does right and be there to praise him.

69

(d) Be understanding, reprimand only when a mistake is made without holding it against the person.

(e) Establish a good recruitment policy so that staffs employed are the staying type. It is common experience that younger people leave jobs quickly and more often than middle-aged people with experience.

(f) Set and example of expected behaviour, because people learn more easily by imitation. For example, a hard working, punctual and dedicated manager tends to nurture a team of workers who follow the same standards in their work. Managing staff well means being one with them, and yet not interfering in their work.

Time

All the work, whatever, its nature, is required to be performed within a restricted period of time. In the catering field where food has to be served at particular times, the pressures build up for staff in kitchens, service and clearing areas, from time to time. Often managers and supervisors have to work long hours to have plans and schedules for jobs ready in advance to enable work to flow as smoothly as possible.

Because of the peaks and troughs of activity that characterize catering operations, a lot of this valuable resource gets wasted, at different points in the production and service cycle. To avoid this it is important to analyse each person's work to determine how well or otherwise time is being utilized. Philip E.

Atkinson has suggested that a way to collect data on time utilization is to maintain a diary of "time log" in which details are recorded showing how time was utilized, by whom, what was the desirable result and any comment on the achievement in that time period against what the objectives for the period were. This could be recorded at regular half or one hour intervals. An accurate record helps to focus attention on time periods, which were used inadequately and during which useful activities could be performed.

If the information has been recorded accurately, an analysis will show the amount of time which may have been spent on:

(i)   Waiting for ingredients, instructions, equipment, maintenance or just looking out of the window between feeding the grating machine and putting the next lot into it.

(ii) Doing other people's jobs because they are absent, or incapable of handling their workload, or simply because of a friendly gesture to a newcomer.

(iii) Doing routine non-creative jobs feeding potatoes into a peeling or chipping machine.

It is surprising how much can come to the surface if each detail is recorded and analysed. Very often staff time is spent doing things they like to do rather than on what they ought to be doing. Sometimes one person has too much to do while others have idle time because of faulty scheduling.

This may also be due to some people being faster than others at work, but then each person's potential would need to be utilized to the maximum possible.

Managers can thus use analysed information to adjust job distribution or content to minimize idle time, build creativity into work by minimizing routineness of jobs through job rotation. This will also enable staff potential in particular job positions to be identified and encouraged.

When there is recorded evidence of time being wasted staff may be involved in presenting suggestions for improvement of time utilization. It is well worth remembering that if a material resource is only half used, the rest can still be used another time, but time wasted is gone and with it the money spent on it too. This resource must therefore never be wasted. As Benjamin

Franklin once said: "... Do not squander time for it is the stuff that life is made have". Once time wasting areas have been pinpointed after a thorough analysis of each person's job, decisions regarding their future use can be made. For the manager these may involve:

(a) A change in management style if too much control and unnecessary interference in routine activities has led to a disinterested work force who idles away productive time deliberately.

(b) Delegation of simple tasks giving greater attention to planning and organization.

(c) Periodic re-evaluation of goals to eliminate activities, which are no more necessary.

(d) Determining training needs and planning them to train staff when required.

(e) Making time and activity plans for each type of job, to give a clear idea of what is expected of people on their jobs.

Time is one factor, which is equally distributed to all people (24 hours a day) irrespective of their educational background, skills and nature of job. But, as Krishnan and Agnihotry have aptly stated "...most of us spend the better part of our lives, not knowing where we want to go and the rest of our lives in extricating ourselves from a self-woven web of confusion."

So a lot of wasted time at operative or production and service levels can be attributed to management inefficiency-either in goal setting or communicating goals to people.

Fortunately, time analysis is simpler at the physical activity level and conditions can be improved through measurements, recording and analysis, and consequent correction of inefficiencies. But, as one goes to line, middle and top management levels, the physical activity related to production and service is gradually replaced by mental activity and assessing this for time utilization is not an easy task. In some cases, time seems short because there is no proper delegation of responsibilities, so there is genuinely too much to do in target time. In other cases, it is simply inefficiently used time that could be corrected to provide greater relaxation, and better output. To maximize utility of time managers need to:

(a) Set clear-cut goals and plan out work sequences in detail.
(b) Trust colleagues and delegate work to subordinates.
(c) Get priorities right so that the most important work is done first and the rest in descending order of importance. This ensures that work that cannot be completed would not matter very much at the end of the day, or could easily be taken up first thing next morning without affecting the work of others.
(d) Develop an easy management style so that people gain confidence in the plan of action laid out for them. Also any work plan that has the participation of those involved in the work helps better commitment to plans and improved performance in target time.
(e) Schedule work among employees so mat their skills are best utilized.

Much time gets wasted when there is too little to do, too much secrecy leading to an unwillingness to delegate work, fear of making mistakes or wrong decisions, too much unnecessary paper work and its storage, too many interruptions through telephone calls, unscheduled visitors, lack of information and poor communication.

Some causes of time wasting in kitchens and service areas, are:

(i) Reaching late to work to subordinates.

(ii) Not having production plans in advance.

(iii) Ingredients not requisitioned in time to start work immediately on arrival.

(iv) Ingredients out of stock because of late ordering or non-availability for some reason,

(v) Equipment not well maintained or not right for the job. For instance, even a small kitchen tool like a kitchen knife, if not sharp enough, will take longer to cut and also require more energy, for cutting meat or vegetables than a well-sharpened knife,

(vi) Conditions of temperature and humidity in working areas being ignored leading to lethargy and slower movement at work. Poor lighting and ventilation are also contributory factors.

(vii) Improperly planned spaces and work centres.

(viii) Not enough motivation or drive to work.

(ix) Some problem within the family or at works, medical, social or psychological.

(x) Ignorance of how the job is to be done.

(xi) Fear of annoying superiors.

(xii) Laziness as a personality trait.

(xiii) Autocratic leadership with excessive supervision and interference in the work.

(xiv) Kitchens too large, leading to much travel time between work centres,

(xv) Too many bosses, leading to confusion about what is to be done and how.

(xvi) Socializing at work, because of lack of loyalty to the organization or lack of devotion to duty. Through a critical time analysis of production, service and management styles therefore, it is possible a control time wasting activities, and save this valuable resource for constructive, planned action and achievement.

Energy

In any discussion of energy it is important to distinguish between the fuel sources used in food services and human effort (energy). Until recently this resource was available in plenty and people did not even link have saving coal, oil or wood, which was commonly used for cooking purposes. In remote areas the powdered coal, which remained after the large pieces were used up, was mixed with cow dung made into cakes or balls and sun-dried for lighting kitchen fires. This does indicate that in areas where sources of fuel were in short supply, there was an inbuilt tendency to use every bit of it either as such, or after recycling it. In shorter, saving sources of energy is a habit more than something that can be taught, although ringing about a change in attitude towards conservation is more feasible when the supplies are dwindling. It is a fact that people's awareness regarding energy saving gets enhanced when the prices of fuels being used rise beyond their means or when there is none available in the market. Today the situation is one of high prices, shortages and sometimes-even non-availability. This statement holds good for both-fuels as well as for catering staff or human effort. Although the latter are available in plenty in the job market, they prefer to choose jobs, which require less effort. This is so also with the people who are educated in colleges and universities who aim at management positions straightaway.

Those with no basic education at all tend to be rejected by the industry or are low paid. Therefore, it is a great challenge for food service institutions to utilize the skills and effort of existing staff to the maximum because, skilled persons would be available only at a substantial price if they have to be recruited and selected too often and then trained to suit requirements. Thus, to make full use of our energy resources, it is important to stop wasting them.

An indication of good utilization of fuel is evident from the overhead expenses of an establishment. The first step in any effort to save fuel in kitchens and service areas is to make staff aware of the costs involved, in concrete terms. This can only be done if action is taken to have separate bills for the kitchen and service areas. The area of wastage can then be identified and further analyses for points of leakage or careless use. This can then be followed up and methods evolved to prevent the loss. Some ways in which fuel energy is wasted in kitchens are:

(a) Keeping ovens, stoves or grills switched on much before they are required for use.

(b) Sometimes cooking range tops are left switched on by mistake when the fuel being burnt is not visible, such as in equipment with solid tops in which a radiant filament is not visible.

(c) Fuel may be wasted if equipment is lighted for full heat irrespective of the size of the container in which the cooking is done.

(d) When the temperature of cooking is higher than is necessary for a particular food, wastage takes place. This is also true for extended periods of cooking, which may not be required.

(e) Foods cooked straight from the freezer without thawing use up more fuel than if thawed in advance.

(f) Non-seasonal foods take longer to cook and therefore consume more fuel than seasonal vegetables, or tender cuts of meat and so on.

(g) Methods of cooking involving preparation of food long before the time of service, require food to be held hot for longer periods. Besides affecting food quality fuel bills go up.

(h) Use of high wattage bulbs in areas where lesser light can do.

(i) Keeping exhaust fans running when kitchens and service areas are not being used.

(j) Using colours on walls and ceilings, and materials that absorb light instead of reflecting it back for good visibility. This leads to the necessity of providing artificial lighting involving the use of electricity, which could otherwise have been saved.

Once the reasons for the high costs of fuel have been established it is possible to improve the situation and bring down costs to the benefit of both the establishment and the customers. The staffs also stand to gain because lower costs and higher productivity mean extra bonuses for them. So far factors affecting fuel energy conservation have been discussed. A look into areas where human effort may be wasted is worthwhile even though the work of people cannot be so closely and objectively monitored as that of physical structural arrangement and equipment. A brief resume of the factors that may affect the amount of energy people waste at work will help as a guideline for necessary action in any programme involving its conservation.

These factors are:

(a) Ill-planned layouts involving extra movement while working, or strain in the performance of certain actions.
(b) Uncomfortable working conditions leading to slow movements, and fatigue.
(c) Poorly scheduled work and time of staff.
(d) Poor health of employees making them feels rundown, and more prone to frequent sickness and accidents.
(e) Aggressive behaviour as a personality trait through which a lot of energy that could be utilized productively gets wasted in destructive activity.
(f) Poor supervision leading to wrong methods of working, using up extra effort and time.
(g) Emergencies where a lot of energy is wasted in panic, fear and anger.

(h) Leadership style that generates fear, anxiety and lack of confidence in people at work.

There is no doubt then, which time and energy need to be conserved for efficient use. Time, if lost, never returns although energy can be regenerated but only at the cost of more energy which is required for the purpose. As far as people are concerned labour costs also go up because most time and energy have to compensate by extra man-hours. It is only right to assume therefore that any methods that help conserve energy should also help to save time as well, leading to greater efficiency. It would therefore be appropriate to list out the possible ways of saving time and energy in a food service establishment suggestions are:

(a) Invest on equipment designed to switch off fuel supply automatically when cooking is Examples are equipment fitted with automatic timers on which a time period is fixed by the who places the dish to be cooked.

(b) Use of thermostats to control temperatures so that higher than necessary temperatures are not for cooking, holding or storing food.

(c) Using the right size of pans for the quantities being prepared, so that fuel is not wasted in heating up larger vessels.

(d) Heating elements and range tops should be switched off when not required. The hot plates may switched off a few minutes before the food is done as it retains heat for some time after it is turn off. Experience with cooking of various dishes enables kitchen staff to judge fairly accurately which food will need to be kept on the source of fuel longer than others. It is now possible to manufacture pan-sensing devices that automatically switch off the fuel source when the pan is lifted from, there cooking range. Similarly warning bells are used to remind staff that a dish in the oven has to be checked. In some cases warning lights may be used.

(e) Arrangement of work centres to avoid extra movements.

(f) Efforts to recycle heat given off from kitchens for purposes of raising the temperature of washing water would conserve lot of fuel.

(g) Arrangement of refrigerators away from kitchens would require less electricity to run them efficiently. Also, condensers of cooling equipment should never face the wall, because the heat released has no outlet and tend to raise the temperature of the environment unduly. Every establishment may find something to add to this list after evaluating their work areas for resource use, because the factors covered are only a guideline from which to proceed. What *is* important is the awareness of the fact that resources are always limited, because wants are unlimited, and therefore the 'best' way to use them should be discovered for each individual establishment.

Procedures

Procedures refer to the methods followed in performing tasks. These have already been referred to under 'Task Analysis'. In large quantity food production and service, certain techniques need to be developed which make-work easier and quicker to perform. The aim of every food service unit should be to follow correct procedures for every job so that the results may be consistent in terms of quality, quantity and time and energy consumption. Some points to pay special attention to while preparing foods for service:

(i) Collect all equipment and ingredients required before starting work to save extra steps.

(ii) Light burners only after all the ingredients are ready for cooking and pans have been placed in position for heating.

(iii)   Extinguish idle flames at once between cooking one item and another.

(iv)   Once boiling starts reduce the flame to maintain at boiling temperature. This results in a fuel saving of nearly 30 per cent,

(v)   The size of the burner or flame should be proportionate to the utensil placed on it. Smaller burners consume 5-6 per cent less fuel, and should be made use of when preparing small quantities of food.

(vi)   Minimum amount of water should be used for cooking to conserve resources.

(vii)   Soak whole cereals and pulses to soften them before cooking to reduce cooking time and fuel.

(viii)   Soak all used utensils immediately after use for quick and easy cleaning. This procedure reduces the quantity of detergent required as well as effort in cleaning,

(ix)   Coating of undissolved salts on the insides of boiling or steaming equipment increases fuel consumption. A good procedure to follow is to clean such equipment regularly with a scrubber to prevent deposits from accumulating in the equipment.

Effective utilisation of resources is matter of good planning organisation and Control.

Four

Overall View of Food Control

Food and beverage control may be defined as the guidance and regulation of the costs and revenue of operating the catering activity in hotels, restaurants, hospitals, schools, employee restaurants and other establishments. The importance of food and beverage control needs considerable emphasis. In hotels, food and beverage sales often account for up to half of the total revenue; The cost of food and beverages in the commercial sector is usually in the region of 25-45 per cent of the total operating costs.

The amount of control is related to the size of the operation. A large group operation obviously requires much precise, detailed, up-to-date information, and its provision is often aided by the used of computers. A small operation, such as an owner-operated the same level of sophistication of control. In both instances the type and volume of data required needs to be selectively determined if control is to be meaningful and effective.

It is important at this stage to clarify the limitations of a control system.

1. A control system in itself will not cure or prevent problems occurring. An effective system is dependent upon correct

up-to-data policies and operational procedures. But the system should identify problems and trends in the business.

2. A control system will required constant management supervision to ensure that it functions efficiently.
3. A control system will need management action to evaluate the information produced and to act upon it.

The Objectives of Food Control

The objects of a food and beverage control system may be summarized as follows:

1. *Analysis of income and expenditure.* The analysis is solely concerned with the income and expenditure related to food and beverage operations. The revenue analysis is usually by each selling outlet, of such aspects as the volume of food and beverage sales, the sales mix, the average spending power of customers at various times of day, and the number of customers served. The analysis of costs included departmental food and beverage costs, portion costs and labour+ costs. The analysis of costs includes departmental food and beverage costs, portion costs and labour costs. The performance of each outlet can then be expressed in terms of the gross profit and the net margin (i.e., gross profit minus swages) and the net profit (i.e., gross profit min use wages and all overhead expenses such as rent, rates, insurance, etc,).

2. *Establishment and maintenance of standards.* The basis for the operation of any food and beverage outlet is the establishment of a set of standards, which would be particular to an operation, for example a chain of steak house restaurants. Unless standards. Unless standards are set no employee would know in detail the standards to be achieved nor could management effectively measure the

employee's performance. An efficient unit would have the set standards laid down in manuals often known as SOPs (standard operational procedures) that should be readily available to all staff of reference. Having set the standards, a difficult problem always for the management of an operation is to maintain these standards. This can be aided by regularly checking on the standards achieved by observation and analysis and by comments made by customers, and when necessary, conducting training courses to re-establish the standards.

3. *Pricing.* An important objective of food an beverage control is to provide a sound basis for menu pricing including quotations for special functions. It is, therefore, important to determine food menu and beverage list prices in the light of accurate food and beverage costs and other main establishment costs; as well as general market considerations, such as the average customer spending power, the prices that the market will accept.

4. *Prevention of waste.* In order to achieve performance standards for an establishment, targets are set for revenue, cost levels and profit margins. To achieve these levels of performance it is necessary to prevent wastage of materials caused by such things as poor preparation, over-production, failure to use standard recipes, etc. This can only be done with an efficient method of control, which covers the complete cycle of food and beverage control, from the basis policies of the organization to the management contrail after the event.

5. *Prevention of fraud.* It is necessary for a control system to prevent or at least restrict the possible areas of fraud by customers and staff. Typical areas of fraud by customers are such things as deliberately walking out without paying; unjustifiably claiming that the food or drink that they had partly or totally consumed was

83

unpalatably claiming that the food or drink that they had partly or totally consumed was unpalatable and indicating that they will not pay for it; disputing the number of drinks served; making payments by stolen cheques or credit cards. Typical areas of fraud by staff are overcharging or undercharging for items served and stealing of food, drink or cash.

6. *Management information.* A system of control has an important task to fulfil ion providing accurate up-to-data information for the preparation of periodical reports for management. This information should be sufficient so as to provide a complete analysis of performance for each outlet of an establishment for comparison with set standards previously laid down (for example, budget standards). The amount of control necessary is related to the size and complexity of an establishment. A small owner—managed restaurant would not require the same level of control and written management information as would a l rage multi-outlet hotel.

Whatever the size and type of operation, the management control information required has to be limited to what is really necessary and meaningful. Therefore some selectivity is necessary to determine what exactly is required, as against producing a mass of statistical information which may be of little use or value and which may well cloud the essential basic data. The speed by which management information can be produced today with the assistance of microcomputers enables corrective action to take place very much quicker than when all the information has to be collected, collated, analysed and presented manually.

A large unit with many selling outlets, employing a large number of staff and producing a large turnover would require quite a sophisticated control system giving often daily reports as well as weekly and periodic reports.

A Small unit such as operated by chef proprietor would required a very simple control system as the proprietor would be involved with controlling all the activates of the unit every day. The proprietor would not only have a 'feel' for all aspects of the business but would also be taking corrective action quickly whenever necessary.

Special Problems of Food Control

Food and beverage control tends to be more difficult than the control of materials in many other industries. The main reasons for this are:

1. The perish ability of the produce. Food, whether raw or cooked, is a perishable commodity and has a limited life. The caterer, therefore, has to ensure that he buys produce in the correct quality and quantity in relation to estimated demand, and that it is correctly stored and processed. (Beverages are normally not as perishable as food and this contributes to their easier control).

2. The unpredictability of the volume of business. Sales instability is typical of most catering establishments. They're often a change in the volume of business from day to day, and in many establishments from hour to hour. This causes basis problems with regard to the quantities of commodities to be purchased and prepared as well as to the staffing required.

3. The unpredictability of the menu mix. To add to the caterer's problems is the fact that in order to be competitive and satisfy a particular market, it is often necessary to offer a wide choice of menu items to the customers. It is therefore necessary to be able to predict not only the number of customers who will be using the facility at particular period in time, but as to what the customer's selection will be form the alternatives offered

on a menu. It is seldom possible to be 100 per cent accurate, but in order to control costs effectively, it is necessary to have some method of volume forecasting as part of the total food and beverage control system.

4. The short cycle of catering operations. The speed at which catering operations take place, relative to many other intestacies, allows little time to many other industries, allows little time for many control tasks. It is not uncommon that items ordered one day are received, that items ordered on day are received, processed and sold the same or next day. It is for this reason that in larger catering establishments cost reporting is done daily or at least weekly. Further problems, particularly with perishable foods, are that with a short life for produce, items cannot be bought very much in advance of their need; and the problem of availability at times of produce relative to the price that can be afforded in relation to the selling price.

5. Departmentalisation. Many catering establishments have several production and service departments, offering different products and operating under different policies. IT is, therefore, necessary to be able to produce separate trading results for each of the production and selling activities.

The Fundamentals of Food Control

Effective control systems and procedures consist of three broad phases: planning, operational, and management control after the event. The planning phase

It is difficult to run an effective catering operation without having firstly defined the basics policies. Policies are predetermined guidelines, laid down by the senior management of an organization, which outline such matters as the market or segment of the market that is being aimed at, how it is to be catered for and the level of profitability/subsidy to be achieved. Policies in general are particular to individual companies and establishments, although in the politic sector operations, there may well be broad national policies, for example for hospital catering.

A catering operation should have its policies clearly defined before it commences business, and redefined whenever a major change taken place, for a restaurant to aim for a different market segment. Ideally, in a large organization the polices should be written down and periodically reviewed in relation to the current business and future trends; however, in smaller organizations there is not the communication problem of a large organization and to formally draw up and commit policies to paper is not so vital.

There are three basic policies, which need to be considered:

1. The financial policy. Will determine the level of profitability, subsidy or cost limits to be expected from the business as a whole and the contribution to the total profit subsidy or cost limit that is to be expected from each unit, and then from the departments within them. This involves the setting of targets for the business as whole as well as each unit and the departments within them. Thus, the financial policy for a large hotel will set profit targets for the accommodation and catering as well as other departments. The financial policy for the catering department will set the overall target for the department itself, which will be further divided into targets for the various restaurants, bars and function facilities. The financial policy for an industrial contract catering operation, the level of subsidy and the level of management fee, as well as the cost limits per unit (meal or employee).

2. The marketing policy will identify the broad market the operation is intended to serve and the particular segments (s) of the market upon which it intends to concentrate. It should also identify the immediate and future consumer requirements on a continuous basis in order to maintain and improve its business performance. It is obvious from the above that the broad market intoned to be served by a large city hotel could be broken down into the specific segments of the various types of users of, for example, the coffee shop, the carver, the cocktail bar, the banqueting rooms, etc. each having specific and different consumer requirements. The interpretation of the marketing polity for a national commercial catering organization into a marketing plan for the next year may include some or all of the following objectives:

   (a) *National identity*—to achieve a better national identity for all units by corporate design, and by meeting consumer expectations of what a 'popular restaurant' concept should be.

   (b) *Customer*—the customer profile being the business person, shopper tourist of either sex, aged twenty-five years or more, commonly using the high street of any major town, requiring food and beverage of good general standard, waitress served, for a typical price of meal.

   (c) *Market share*—to achieve, maintain or increase the percentage of 'our' market.

   (d) *Turnover*—sales volume to be increased by x per cent on previous year.

   (e) *Profitability*—profit to be increased by each unit by percent on previous year.

   (f) *Product*—The product to be maintained at a consistently high standard.

   (g) *Customer satisfaction*—the net result must be the satisfaction of every customer.

3. The Catering policy, which is normally evolved from the financial and marketing policies, will define the main o objectives of operating the food and beverage facilities and describe the methods by which such objectives are to be achieved. It will usually include the following:

   (a) The type of customer, for example high spending business executive, low spending female shopper, short-stay hospital patient, etc.

   (b) The type of menu(s), for example table d' hotel'a la cart, fast food,

   (c) The beverage provision necessary for the operation.

   (d) The food quality standards, for example fresh, frozen, canned, etc., and the grade of produce to be used.

   (e) The method of buying, for example by contract, quotation, cash-and-carry, etc.

   (f) Type and quality of service, for example cafeteria, counter, waiter, etc.

   (g) Degree of comfort and décor, for example square footage per customer, type and style of décor, of chairs, tables etc.

   (h) Hours of operation, for example twenty-four hours, seven days a week: 1200-1500 and 1800-2200 hours, Monday-Saturday, etc.

The Operation Phase

Having defined the policies (that is, predetermined guide lines), it is then necessary to outline how they are to be interpreted into the day-today control activities of the catering operation. The operational control is in five main stage of the control cycle. These are:

1. *Purchasing*—There are five main points to be considered.

   (a) *Product testing*—to identify as a result of a series of taste panel evaluations the particular products to be used.

    (b) *Yield testing*—to identify as a result of tests the yield obtainable from all the major commodities used.

    (c) *Purchase specifications*—a specification is a concise description in writing of the quality, size, weight, etc, for a particular food ob beverage item.

    (d) *Method of buying*—by contract, quotation, cash and carry, etc.

    (e) *Clerical procedures*—it is necessary to determine who originates, sanctions and places orders and what documentation is required for control.

2. *Storing and issuing*—There are four main point to be considered:

    (a) *Stock records*—it is necessary to decide with records are to be kept.

    (b) *Pricing of issues*—the method of pricing of the various types of issues must be decided upon so that there is consistency within the operation. Although there are many ways to price issues, it is common to use one or more of these methods: actual purchase price: selling price: simple average price: weighted average price;

    (c) *Stocktaking*—the points to be considered here are the level of stock to be held; rate of stock turnover dealing

    (d) Clerical *procedures*—there is a need to determine what documentation is necessary, for example requisitions, record cards, being cards, stocktaking reports, etc.

3. *Preparing*—This is a critical stage in the control cycle, in particular for food. There are three main points to be considered:

    (a) *Volume forecasting*—a method of predicting the member of customers using the catering facilities on a specific day, and also of predicting as accurately as possible what items they will eat and drink.

(b) *Pre-costing*—a method of controlling food and beverage costs in advance of the preparation and service stage. It is done pay preparing and using standard recipes for all food and beverage items and also by using portion control equipment, for example ladles, scales, optics, standard glassware, etc.

(c) *Clerical procedures*—what documentation is required and the distribution and destination of this information.

4. *Selling*—This important stage of operational control needs to take into consideration the following points:

(a) *A checking system*—this is necessary to keep control of the number of covers sold and of the items sold. This may be done through a standard type of waiter's check system or through a till roll or in the case of hospital patients, by the summary and analysis of completed individual patient menu cards.

(b) *The control of cash*—this is vitally important. It is necessary to ensure that all items sold have been paid for and that the money is received or credit has been authorized.

This final phase of food and beverage control is in three main stages:

1. *Food and beverage cost reporting*—As mentioned earlier in this chapter, the cycle of production is very short and the product is perishable. These factors together with the variations in demand for the product necessitate up-to-date reporting at least weekly if not daily.

2. *Assessment*—There is a need for someone from the food and beverage management term in the case of a large unit, or the proprietor or manager of a small unit, to analyses the food and beverage reports and to compare

them with the budget for the period and against previous actual performance.

3. *Correction*—A control system does to cure or prevent problems occurring. When the analysis of the performance of a unit or

The Reality of Food Control

As has been stated earlier in this chapter, the amount of control necessary is related to the size and complexity of an operation. The larger the number of outlets within an operation, the more sophisticated should be the level of control

However, it is important for the reader to realize the extent to which any control system can be totally efficient.

In reality no control system will be 100 per cent efficient for such basic reasons as:

1. The material product (apart from purchased beverages) is very unlikely to be 100 per cent consistent as to quality or the final yield obtainable from it.
2. The staff employed are unlikely to work to a level of 100 per cent efficiency at all times, in spite of the fact that operational manuals may exist.
3. The equipment used is also unlikely to work to the level of 100 per cent efficiency and this could well affect the yield obtainable.
4. The customers' choice of dishes can well be different at times to some of the budgeted sales mix, therefore affecting all production forecasts as well as the average spend per customer and the budgeted gross and net profit figures. It is terribly important that the staff should see that control in some form is taking place and that on occasions there is a follow-up and action is taken on irregularities to set standards.

Five

Food Controlling

The main objectives of food cost control are

1. The analysis of income and expenditure.
2. The establishment and maintenance of standards.
3. The pricing and quotations of menus
4. The prevention of waste.
5. The prevention of fraud.
6. Information for management reports.

The Essentials of Control System

It is important when examining an existing control system or preparing to install a system into a new operation that the following points should be borne in mind.

1. Any control system should be comprehensive and cover all the outlets of an establishment and all stages of the food control cycle.
2. The cost of maintaining the system should be in relation to the saving to be made, the level of sophistication of the control system usually increasing with the increase in

the volume of sales and the complexity of the menu.
3. The control system should be easy to operate and to be understood by all levels of staff.
4. The control system should be seen by staff to be working. That is, that management act in a positive way to adverse trading results and follow up on future results to check if the corrective action taken is effective.
5. To be effective the information produced must be accurate and up-to-date.

Calculation of Food Cost

There are several basic terms which need to be emphasized with regard to the calculation of food costs, such as:

1. *Food cost.* This refers to the cost of food incurred in preparing the meals served.
2. *Food cost percentage.* Refers to the percentage of the revenue from sales incurred in preparing the meals, that is, of the food as a percentage of sales of food.
3. *Gross profit or kitchen gross profits.* The excess of sales over the cost of food expressed as a percentage, or in financial terms.
4. *Potential food cost or sales.* The food cost (or sales) under perfect conditions. This may be expressed as a percentage or in financial terms.

Methods of Food Control

Weekly/Monthly Food Cost Report

The following is an example for the calculating of the monthly food costs for an operation where detailed information is not thought to be necessary, or for a small or owner-managed unit where the control is an everyday part of the manager's activity in order for the operation to be successful. The weekly/monthly food cost report is almost a reconciliation report on activity that is tightly controlled daily by management.

The Advantages of this Methods are:
1. It is simple and quick to produce.
2. It can give an indication of the general performance of the unit.

The Disadvantages though are:
1. This information only produced after seven or twenty-eight days of operation.
2. It provides no intermediate information so that any undesirable trends (for example, food costs too high) may be corrected earlier.
3. It does not provide the daily or to-date information on purchase, requisitions and sales that a unit with an average of •1,000 a day turnover should.

A Daily Food Cost Report

This food cost method is suitable for a small-to medium-sized operation, or one where a not too sophisticated method is required, or where the costs involved in relation to the savings to be made do not justify a more involved method.

The following is a step-by-step procedure on compromising the report.

Prepare a chart on column paper and complete entries on ka day-to-day basis as follows:

1. It is simple and easy to follow.
2. It gives a detailed account of the general performance of the business on a day-to-day bias.
3. It records the daily stock level, daily purchases, daily food requisitioned and daily food sales and enables the

daily food cost percentage to be calculated. This information is used for preparing to-date totals (that is, running totals to date).

4. Up-to-date food cost percentage smooth out the uneven daily food cost percentages and highlights the corrective action to e taken, if daily food cost percentage is often caused when food is requisitioned on one day to be processed and sold on subsequent days.

The disadvantages of this basics food report are:

1. Although simple and easy to prepare, the report relies heavily on the accuracy of the basic information to be collected, for example the total of daily purchases, daily requisitions, etc.

2. It is not totally accurate as it ignores such things as the cost of the staff meals; food transferred to bars, for example potato crisps, nests, salted biscuits, trays of canapés, etc. which are given away free in the bars to customers and items such as lemons, limes, etc. which are included in certain drinks and beverages transferred to kitchens, for example wine, spirits, beer, etc. for use in the cooking of specific dishes.

A Detailed Daily Food Cost Report

This food cost report is a development of the previous report and refines the accuracy of the report by taking into account the cost of beverages transferred into the kitchen, the cost of food transferred out of the kitchens to the bars, and the cost of employees' meals.

1. It includes additions to the cost of food for beverages transferred to the kitchen and deductions for the cost of food transferred from the kitchen to the bars and for the

cost of all employees' meal. It also separates purchases into those that go straight to the storerooms and those that go direct to the kitchen and are charged immediately to the kitchen. The result of these additions and subtractions is that the true cost of the food sold to customers is more accurate than previously.

2. The accuracy of the to-date food cost percentage is refined to take into account all daily transactions and these figures should be fully relied upon to be the basis against which corrective action may be taken.

The disadvantages of this type of report are that it is more detailed than the previous reports and it relies very much on the accuracy of the collected information, for example the collection of all the requisition notes and the accurate extensions of the pricing of items; the collection of the goods received sheet and the checking of it against delivery notes, credit notes, invoices, etc.

Calculation of the Potential Food Cost

The potential food cost is the cost of the food under perfect and ideal conditions. The potential food cost of an operation is the principal and most effective method of evaluating the actual food cost. Any variance higher than 1 percent between the potential and actual costs should be investigated. The potential food cost may be calculated in a variety of ways, but because of time is it is usually coasted per menu for each selling outlet twice a year or more frequently if the menu changes.

Begin by entering the opening stock value (that is, the closing stock value at the end of the last period). On subsequent days enter in this column the difference between column 5 and column 6 of the previous.

Enter the total of all goods purchased and received on that day.

Total of all goods requisitioned by the chef on that day.

Total food sales as recorded by the cashier/manager and will consist often of cash plus credit accounts.

To-date total of all food purchases, that is, the sum total of all purchasing for the period to date.

To-date total of all food sales for the period.

The advantages of producing this basic food report are:

1. It is simple and easy to follow.
2. It gives a detailed account of the general performance of the business on a day-to-day bias.

The disadvantages of this basics food report are:

1. For each individual menu item multiply the number of portions actually sold during a 'sample' week as determined by the restaurant sales analysis, by the potential food cost per portion to obtain the total potential cost of food sold for that week.
2. Multiply the same portions actually sold, as above, by the menu selling prices, and arrive at the potential total sales.
3. Divide the potential total food cost by the potential total food sales and arrive at a figure which, when expressed as a percentage, is the potential food cost percentage. To be able to do the above calculations it would be necessary to have the following information to hand.

It is not unusual for there to be a difference between the actual and the potential food cost figures. Usually the actual cost of the food sold is higher than the potential for such reasons as food being a perishable commodity, the difficulty of being exact when forecasting food production requirements and that a small amount of waste is almost unavoidable. Any large difference to established standards, or pilfering of sheer carelessness resulting in an excessive amount of waste. As stated earlier, any variance in excess of 1 per cent should be investigated

Food Control Checklist

It would not be possible to state in a book what corrective action should be taken when standards are not being met, as the operating and trading conditions would vary from one establishment to another.

It is possible, however, to produce a control checklist, similar to the one below, to act as *an aid-memoir* when trying to identify the reasons for any variance in standards, the reasons for any variance in standards the checklist being a summary of the control procedures, which should be used. Any control procedures not being used would be a weak link in the chain of control.

Menu

1. Suitable for present market segment.
2. Takes into account current trends in customer eating habits.
3. Menu is interesting, imaginative, changes during the year, takes into account the major food seasons, assists greatly in selling.
4. Accurately priced, competitive, take into account the labour content in the production and service of dishes.

Purchasing, Receiving, Storing and Issuing Procedures

1. Purchase specifications used for all main items.
2. Purchase orders made for every purchase the exception

possibly being to the daily order of fresh fruit and vegetables.

3. All purchases made from nominated or approved suppliers.

4. Deliveries timetabled whenever possible so that quantity and quality checks may be efficiently carried out.

5. All deliveries to be recorded in the foods received book and credit notes obtained for any variance between what is stated on the delivery note and what is actually delivered.

6. All deliveries of food to be entered into bin cards/ledgers on the day of delivery.

7. Issues of all food from the stores to be against authorized, signed requisitions only.

8. Entry to food stores to be restricted to authorized personnel.

Food Production

1. Yield and product testing practiced to establish and measure standards of products.

2. Production to be related to volume forecasts.

3. Maximum use to be made of standards recipes.

4. Efficient scheduling of production to be made so as to ensure eminences of quality of dishes produced.

5. All equipment to be regularly maintained so as to ensure the standard yields as quality of dishes is maintained.

Food Service

1. Food services standards established and practiced.

2. Standards portion sizes adhered to.

3. Standard portion size equipment always available.

4. Careful control made to all food sent to restaurant, for example sweet and carving trolleys, etc. All unsold food to be accounted for and returned to the kitchen.

Food Control Procedures

1. Check and marry up all delivery notes, invoices and goods received report.
2. Check arithmetic to all paper work.
3. Check correct discounts are being allowed.
4. Check delivery notes to bin cards/ledgers.
5. Maintain certain charges and credits for period inventory.
6. At set periods complete a full inventory of all chargeable containers.
7. At set periods complete a full stocktaking of all food stores and food held in the kitchens and compare to ledgers.
8. Prepare a stocktaking stocktaking report and stocktaking variance report.
9. Maintain up-to-date food control reports.

The major reasons for food cost (and gross profit) variances from the established standards for a unit include the following.

1. Inaccurate arithmetic to paperwork. This also includes the paperwork of suppliers.
2. Inefficient stocktaking.
3. Poor revenue control. Lack of systematic procedures and practices.
4. Poor menu. Unrelated to market conditions and requirements, lack of sales analysis and up dating of menu.
5. Poor purchasing, resulting in higher food costs, overstocking and wastage.
6. Poor receiving, inferior goods being accepted, short weight of goods being accepted, short weight of goods being signed for.
7. Poor storing, poor rotation of stock resulting in wastage, poor security.
8. Failure to establish and/or maintain standards for volume

forecasting, standards recipes, standards yields and standards portion sizes.

9. Failure to account accurately for all staff managements.
10. Food controls not being seen by staff to work, resulting in staff failing to maintain desired standards.

Checklist for the Smaller Operation

A quick checklist for the smaller operation for food cost (and gross profit) variances from the established standard would include the following.

1. Check the arithmetic of all major figures (that is, food report, stock report, etc.)
2. Re-check stock figures and total, and in particular look for unusual figures in relation to the norm. The percentage of the total consumption of each category of commodities. (meat, poultry, fish, dairy, fresh vegetables, etc). Should be constant for any given menu over a period. Once a standard has been established, variations from it will indicate a problem, for example if the meat consumption percentage was up it could well indicate pilferage, fraud, wastage or an increases in price and management attention should be focused towards this.
3. Re-check sales figures and check against meals served.
4. Check for unusual variances in sales. A major could cause this change in the weather, a national holiday, etc.
5. Check for unusual changes in the sales mix.
6. Check for unusual changes in price of major and costly food items.
7. Check stores, refrigerators and waste bins for evidence of over purchasing, over preparation and unnecessary wastage.
8. Check on meals taken by staff.

Six

Financial Management: Definition and Scope

Introduction

A few decades ago financial management was thought of as mere bookkeeping and accounting. Today, financial management is also concerned with the manner in which funds are procured for and used in a business. It has therefore an important role to play in making decisions concerning investment, operations and disposition. Financial management techniques are now applied to decisions for individuals as well as for organisations whether they are profit making or non-profit-making. It has become an integral part of management in any sphere.

In any operation financial decision-making involves three aspects:

(i) Funding
(ii) Investing in assets
(iii) Controlling operations

These aspects need to be coordinated in every organization to make effective use of resources.

This unit deals primarily with the scope of financial management as applied to catering establishments, along with a glimpse of some no conventional accounting techniques, which have become essential to enable managers to cope with the cost control pressures of the business environment of today.

As the term indicates, 'financial management' is that area of a business that deals with the effective management of all the resources of an establishment in monetary terms. It not only involves keeping accounts for all the transactions made, but also recording any information in a manner that helps management to make decisions regarding premises, equipment, employees, purchasing, sales, and so on.

This leads 'management accounting' and us to the often-used terms 'accountancy'. 'Accountancy' is used to describe the process of measuring in financial terms, the past, present and future operations of a business. It helps to assess the financial status of an organization at any particular point in time. There term 'management accounting' covers more than just the preparation of financial statements or accounting reports. It is concerned with the interpretation, of the reports and their presentation in a form that will enable managements to make profitable decisions regarding deployment of resources.

Financial management, therefore, covers two basic aspects financial accounting and management accounting. The purpose of financial accounting is to pass on relevant information to agencies outside the establishment for purposes of decision-making. For example, if the organization needs to borrow money for expansion, from a bank, the latter would need information regarding the credibility of the establishment. Again, every business organization needs to provide financial information to income tax authorities or other governmental agencies that can then assess the amount of tax payable. The two statements on which the establishment's soundness can be judged are the balance sheet and the income statement, which give relevant information regarding the increase in the assets of an organization, or its failure to do so. All financial accounting is based on five main concepts:

(a) The entity concept: This refers to the establishment being a specific unit of accountability. The identity of the business is separate from that of the proprietor. Financial accounting is done for the establishment and not for the proprietor. All transactions are thus undertaken on behalf of the establishment.

(b) The concept of going concern: This concept implies that the business is a continuing entity in the sense that its activities are not wound up at the end of the financial period. The financial statement prepared by every establishment enables management to review previous performance in terms of profitability and financial soundness.

(c) The cost concept: This is the monetary unit concept and expresses transactions of an organization in rupees, pounds, dollars, etc. This concept assumes, however, that the purchasing power of the monetary unit is relatively stable from one accounting period to another. Thus, when a transaction is completed it can be recorded as an actual cost.

(d) The concept *of realization:* According to this concept, the revenue is said to have been realized when goods and services are delivered, irrespective of the timing of the payments or receipts in cash.

(e) The accrual concept: According to this concept revenue accrues when it results in a net increase in capital because of transactions, that is, those involving trade exchange of goods and services. Managerial accounting, on the other hand, is meant to provide information on the day-to-day operations of the organisation to managers who have to make decisions regarding the use of resources.

Unlike historical accounting, management accounting is a matter of attitude and approach, though based on knowledge of basic accounting techniques; it also appreciates the complex nature of business problems. Below are some of the facets of management accounting that indicate the scope of the subject and it's utility in running catering operations.

(a) *Cost accounting*: This includes the preparation of cost statements and cost estimates identifying direct and indirect costs involved in the process of production.

(b) *Standard costing*: This is a means of establishing 'standard costs' for every type of resource used, with the help of time and motion studies and research and development. Standard costing also includes comparison of actual with standards and determines any variances arising in the production process. In catering the importance of standard costing for dishes, meals and functions cannot be under emphasized.

(c) *Materials control*: This involves planning and control of stocks to determine the extent of use of materials.

(d) *Budgetary control*: This is the preparation of fixed and flexible budgets, capital and operating budgets, used as standards for measuring actual performance.

(e) *Interpreting statements:* This the preparation of monthly or quarterly profit and loss and position statements, together with information on operating ratios and orders at hand.

(f) *The accounting system:* The establishment of the most appropriate system of maintaining accounts for a food service organization is an important part of the management accounting function. This would involve determination of the books of account to be maintained, the procedures most suitable for collating data and preparing management information, decisions regarding use of mechanical or electronic equipment depending on the volume of the data and the speed with which it is required for decision making.

(g) *Special studies:* This refers to conducting studies relating to cost-volume-profit analysis; break-even analysis and liabilities, so that a sound basis is established for investment decisions. A study of government policies in respect of licensing, taxation, minimum wage and so on is also imperative.

(h) *Financial reports:* These are used by management accountants to provide assistance to managers in the form of offering advice on the most profitable courses of action.

Application of Management Accounting to Catering Operations

Catering being essentially a service industry it has certain special features that make it different from other industries and, therefore, more complex to assess in terms of financial viability. These features are:

1. There is a wide variation in the types of products and services offered to customers, such a food beverages, package services for parties, conferences, etc. The latter include arrangements for decorations, stationery, and microphones and like, activities absolutely unrelated to the preparation and service of food. In addition, it may include accommodation as in college hostels, homes for the handicapped or aged or in other social institutions.

2. There is a large variety of cost incurred by each of the services.

3. The proportion of fixed costs is very high as they continue to be incurred whether the services are used or not.

4. A variety of prices have to be calculated for the same

commodities, depending on the combination of services offered to the customer. For example, the menu served to residents would be charged at a different rate than for guests in a hostel. The same menu if served for a conference lunch or a ladies' party would carry a different charge depending on the cost of extra service staff required, better quality tableware or more expensive garnishing to be used. The additional costs would necessarily be reflected in the price.

5. There is a constant need to price competitively while still maintaining standards and, at the same time, knowing the costs involved for providing products and services profitably.

6 Catering establishments are always subject to seasonal demand for their products and services. Besides seasonal variations and availability in food items, 'mood' of the customer and his paying power also easily affects trading.

7. One product or service can be more profitable than another, yet the latter cannot be dispensed with because of the need to maintain the 'goodwill' of the customer.

8. The product is consumed generally at the point of production, and therefore cannot be overproduced and stored for future sale like in other industries.

9. Catering deals continuously with a large proportion of highly perishable raw and prepared products, so profit 'leaks' are easy through spoilage.

10. Foods also provide excellent media for growth of microorganisms and therefore, if not handled with care, can be a potential health hazard.

All these diverse characteristics make financial management of foodservices a 'tricky' and rather difficult job. Further, catering is not only a labour intensive but also a capital-intensive industry, involving large investments in space, building and equipment.

Decisions are therefore required to make at every stage, which would affect the future deployment of resources. For these decisions to be made effectively, an understanding of accounting information is necessary, which is the basis of 'management accounting'.

Irrespective of the size of the catering operation, accounting reports are useful, because they provide information of the quantities and manner in which resources have been used in the past and whether profitably or not. Knowledge of the relationships of resources to each other and their reactions to environmental changes equips managers of food services to predict the effects of resource use in the future. The importance of analysis sheets pertaining to costs, sales, production, etc. has been further discussed in this unit.

It is thus clear, that those persons who are in charge of controlling resources at each point of food preparation and service, such as the delivery and storage point, preparation and cooking areas and during service, or those who own the resources or consider buying or selling them, can make use of accounting information to make wise decisions. For example, at the ordering stage, decisions regarding buying quantities have to be made. Past reports of inventory can indicate the quantities of particular commodities that have been used and their rate of turnover from stores to user departments. It might be argued that in small establishments large quantities are not required to be stored, because of limited menus and storage spaces. But decisions have still to be made regarding purchase, and some quantities are appreciably cheaper to purchase than others. For instance, buying eggs in trays or in hundreds from a farm located close by (space and funds permitting) may be far cheaper than buying by the dozen from the market according to customer demand.

Again decisions pertaining to the purchase of equipment have to be made even by small establishments. In catering, the decisions regarding equipment purchase depend not only on price or the initial investment required, but on the expected life of the equipment, efficiency in operation, effectiveness in terms of reducing labour costs, and so on. All such information and necessary advice for deciding on the purchase of a particular model or size can be had from wage and investment reports.

If the case of environmental factors resulting in the movement of an establishment from one area to another, decisions regarding selling and buying of premises should be based on techniques for assessing capital projects. These are only possible through accounting information, which figuratively sets out the assets and liabilities involved, and various ratios for making comparisons and judging the profit potential of a new investment.

If the resource involved is a simple one like 'money', a person can measure it himself by simply counting it. But when it comes to a complicated one like a building, machinery or a legal right, then the accountant's report becomes important. Accurately recorded financial information helps management to identify the quantifiable feature of the operation, and measure the extent to which changes have occurred during an accounting period in comparison to previous figures. It then becomes possible to assess the profit or loss incurred over the period in question, and identify those factors responsible for any changes.

Financial control is one of the most important forms of control in any food service operation, because it helps to focus on any lapses that might have occurred in the control process along the line of production and service. For example, an accounting statement showing a lowered net profit in one area of the service can draw management attention towards that particular area. It may have been that meat dishes were just not selling during a particular period of time. The reason could be that at certain times of the year, due to religious reasons. Hindus do not eat meat, and although the number of covers sold remained the same, the sales revenue decreased bringing down profits too.

The applicability of management accounting is of special significance where the financial interests of the catering establishment are involved, because this area deals with all the aspects like building, machinery, sharp tools, processes and, most of all, people, who have to be protected against any sort of hazards. More important, people today, staff and customers, are aware of their rights and without attention to these the food service cannot survive.

Although the importance of financial information has been emphasized, it is well to caution that statements or figures seen in isolation have little significance. It is necessary to relate the information to that of technical, staff and materials controls, to make it meaningful for making profitable decisions.

The accounting process is almost a continuous one, because of the wide range of services and products offered for sale in catering operations. The reports presented generate new choices and ideas for management, helping them to pick up customer tastes and trends quickly and develop future targets realistically.

For any future planning, management needs to know the current status of the establishment in order to be able to evaluate the resources available for channelisation into various courses of action. A framework is also required for predicting the effects of decisions being taken for the future and making valid assumptions about future events. Besides, it is useful to have a basis for studying the cause and effect relationships between environmental factors and the establishment. This helps to build flexibility into the operation. For example, a news report stating that animal fat is being incorporated in the manufacture of hydrogenated cooking fat in India, affects the food services immediately. With a vast majority being vegetarian in India, there suspicions regarding the fats being used for cooking in public eating-places would prevent them from eating out.

A shrewd manager, however, would immediately react to the situation, and put up signs outside his food service saying 'only vegetable cooking oils used' and limit their use of the hydrogenated fat held in stock for cooking of meat dishes only.

A number of examples of the usefulness of cause and effect studies have been cited. It is only accounting information that can help to establish authentic information regarding current status or provides the necessary framework for decision-making.

A uniform system of accounting has been followed by most catering establishments in the West, but with a large number of disorganized establishments mushrooming in the developing countries, a disparity in the methods of maintaining accounts exists.

While accounting is an indispensable tool of management, it also makes the caterer aware of the standing of his operation in comparison to the average for other similar operations. Besides, records can help to see at a glance the performance of each area of the service, and constant comparisons help to improve resource allocation, shifting them from areas of low profit to those of higher ones.

With the development of the management accounting concept, it is now possible to have relevant financial information in a readily understandable form for use in making decisions. Production managers today do not accept the old-time view of the accountant as their controller. The emphasis is gradually shifting to 'Just in Time' (JIT) techniques of managing inventory, in an effort to minimize costs and gain a competitive advantage in the ever-changing catering environment.

There are three types of decisions made in the catering field: (a) Investment decisions; (b) Operational decisions, and (c) Disposition decisions.

Investment Decisions

Investment decisions are concerned with the use of capital, which may or may not belong to the owners of the establishment.

Decisions on capital investments must therefore, ensure a regular return through optimum utilization. It is here that proper techniques of assessment of capital projects in terms, of their assets and liabilities are useful. Changing, taxation policies of the government have their effects on capital investments of an establishment, and its resulting profitability. Sometimes a caterer may find he has accumulated cash balances that are not required for current operational purposes.

He is then faced with an investment decision to be made from a number of choices open to him. He may:

(i)   Consider expanding existing facilities to extend the present services.

(ii) Take over other premises and form a chain of services.

(iii) Decide to modernise existing facilities.

It is in such circumstances that the caterer needs to assess each choice in monetary terms; and to arrive at the most suitable decision he requires accounting reports. There are three main methods of assessing capital projects.

(i)   *The pay back method*: This estimates the time period in years required for a project to pay for itself out of the additional profits it will bring in.

(ii) *The return on investment method*: This method concentrates on the percentage return on investment, that is, net profit before tax on capital cost of a project. The choice would be based on that project which gives the highest percentage return in a given period of time.

(iii) *Discounted cash flow or DCF method:* In this method the value of the cash to be received in the future is lowered to determine its present day value and vice versa, at a given rate of interest. These can be calculated with the help of annuity and present worth tables. The higher the interest rates the lower is the present day value of any amount receivable at a future date. After making adjustments in the future cash inflows, the costs of the projects can be compared more realistically. Where the discounted cash inflow is less than the cost of the project, it is clearly no use undertaking it. The greater the D.C.F. over the cost of the project the more its profitability. Since capital investments commit large sums of money for long periods of time, decisions on them need to be taken after careful scrutiny of detailed accounting information.

Operational Decisions

Those decisions concerned with existing resources and their utilization are known as operational decisions. For instance, decisions pertaining to the sale of food, cost of production, staff costs, overheads and other direct and indirect costs of meals and services offered to the customer, would all be classed as operational.

Disposition Decisions

These are decisions connected with the determination of prices at which products and services will be sold. For example, determining the percentage of profit to be added to the cost of production, so that the prices cover both costs and reasonable profit. It also involves decisions regarding the mode of payment such as, selling on 'strictly cash' terms, or offering facilities for credit by which customers can pay at a later date.

Accounting helps in making such decisions, by informing management about the existing number of debtors and creditors; the amount of cash involved and the value of bad debts.

Disposition decisions are necessary in catering because the level of operational resources is relatively low compared to the higher fixed assets. Also the industry has to cope with constant changes in demand for food and accommodation; keep in touch with technological improvements, while also taking care of the competitive forces in the environment that tend to erode profits.

While the last two decades have seen greater attention focused on the application of accounting techniques to the special needs of catering establishments, it must be remembered that the mechanics of accounting are only a means to an end.

For the smaller establishments, financial results chiefly measure the success of the operation. As the establishments become larger, and greater degree of organization is necessary, financial information becomes crucial to decision making.

Seven

Cost Concepts

In catering a cost may be defined as the price of goods used up, sold or consumed, and services rendered. Items are to be consumed even when they are wasted, stolen or discarded, as happens frequently in food services. This is because they are no longer available for the purpose for which they were purchased. The effort of every establishment is to maximize its profits, and to do that, costs would have to be minimized. To be able to exercise any control on costs therefore, it is important to understand some of the basic concepts underlying them.

Components of Costs

In every food service, there are basically three types of costs involved in its day-to-day operation:

(i) *Cost of materials.* This includes raw food and other ingredients that make up a dish, meal or a beverage, and is commonly referred to as 'material or food cost'.

(ii) *Cost of employees:* This includes the salaries of staff and the value of all benefits provided to them such as meals, housing, medical facilities, uniforms, insurance, bonuses, pensions, etc. It is generally referred to as 'labour or payroll costs'.

(iii) *Overhead cost:* This includes all such costs that cannot be directly identified with food products, such as rent, rates, depreciation, fuel, cleaning materials, administrative and selling costs. These three categories of costs are known as the 'components of cost'. While these give some idea of the nature of cost distribution, they do not tell us what happens to each of these components when there is a drop or an increase in the sales of an establishment. Yet, we know that some of these elements get affected and do change periodically to give different levels of profit.

Behaviour of Costs

The manner in which costs respond to changes in the volume of sales is referred to as the 'behaviour of costs'. To understand how costs behave in various situations, all costs have been placed into one of the three following categories.

Fixed Costs

As the name suggests, these costs remain virtually unaffected by changes in the volume of business of an establishment. Examples of such costs are rents, rates, insurance, and so on. It may be argued that even these are subject to change, but for purposes of assessment of profitability, they remain fixed over a period of time. And, since these costs are paid generally on an annual basis, they remain unchanged over an accounting period as far as the establishment is concerned.

Semi-fixed Costs

These may also be termed as 'semi-variable costs', if the variable component is greater than the fixed element. The extent of variability differs with each cost and in particular circumstances. For example, when feeding more customers the fuel costs change very little compared to a situation in which the menu is changed to include extra frying in preparation. On the contrary, if the menu is changed to include more items requiring no cooking, such as salads and raitas, the fuel costs may actually be reduced for the same number of customers. Again the cost of cleaning materials may be reduced with increase in demand, if disposable tableware and crockery are used. Semi-fixed or semi-variable costs therefore include costs of fuel, cleaning materials, replacements, etc. and change with the output, but not in direct proportion. It is common experience that if more meals are prepared and served (indicating increased turnover) the gas or other fuel used to cook them will increase but not as much as the increase in the output.

Variable Costs

These include food costs, which change in direct proportion to the output. In a food service establishment known for its standards, one would not expect portion sizes to be reduced if, demand for meals goes up, and therefore, it stands to reason that for each extra meal demanded the amount of food materials will increase in the same proportion. In practice however, it may be noted that actual variable costs tend to decrease as the volume increases, because food purchasing in bulk can reduce costs, and labour too becomes more productive with grater time utilization. However, costs fluctuate considerably in catering for several reasons:

(a) Most food costs change seasonally depending on supply and demand conditions.

(b) Inflationary trends affect prices of food and ingredients consistently upwards.

(c) Legislated minimum wage rates and negotiated labour agreements affect labour costs over time. All the above factors need to be anticipated and considered by managers while planning future costs of the establishment and price fixation policies.

Having established the nature and behaviour of costs, every food service manager would be concerned with the effect that his costs will have on profitability. Example illustrates such effects, and gives managers an insight to those elements of costs that may affect their profits adversely.

Example

The sales revenue, costs and profits of two coffee shops is assumed to be as follows:

	A (Rs.)	% turnover	B (Rs.)	% turnover
Variable costs	5000	50	3000	30
Fixed costs	4000	40	6000	60
Net profit	1000	10	1000	10
	10000	100	10000	100

It would be observed that both coffee shops have made an equivalent amount of profit (10 per cent), in spite of different cost structures. To see the effect on profits of change in turnover, let us assume that there has been an increase of 10 per cent in the turnover.

It will be seen that the 10 per cent increase in turnover has increased the profits of the two establishments by 3.6 and 5.5 per cent respectively. The differences may be attributed to the lower increase in the variable costs of *B* (only Rs. 300) as against the variable costs of *A* (Rs. 500) and hence the corresponding higher net profit in *B*.

If there was a decrease in the turnover by 10 per cent the effects would have been as shown below:

	A (Rs.)	% turnover	B (Rs.)	% turnover
Variable costs	4500	50	2700	30
Fixed costs	4000	44.4	6000	66.7
Net profit	500	5.6	300	3.3
	9000	100	1100	100

In this case a decrease of 10 per cent in turnover has reduced the profit of *A* by 50 per cent (from Rs. 1,000 to Rs. 500) and the net profit of *B* by 70 per cent (from Rs. 1,000 to Rs. 300). The managers of the two coffee shops can therefore conclude that:

(i) Any given change in turnover will not lead to a proportionate change in costs.

(ii) Net profit tends to increase or decrease, more than in proportion to an increase or decrease in turnover.

(iii) The higher the fixed cost the greater is the effect on profit or loss for given change in sales volume.

Although increase in sales volume increases total variable costs proportionately, the cost per unit of sale remains constant. This is proved by the fact that all customers irrespective of the numbers on a particular day, pay the same for a particular meal.

This is, however, not the situation as far as fixed costs go. While these costs remain the same whatever the sales volume, the fixed costs per unit decrease when sales volume increases. The following example illustrates these effects.

Example

The fixed costs of a canteen serving 4,000 to 5,000 meals a month are Rs. 3,000 every month. The average amount spent by customers is Rs. 1.50 per meal, of which the food cost (variable cost) per meal is Rs. 0.80 or 80 paise. Find the total cost and net profit or loss per meal when the canteen serves 4,000, 4,200, 4,400, 4,600, 4,800, and 5,000 meals per month.

Total cost and net profit or loss per meal Number of meals served per month

Meals per month	Price per meal (Rs.)	Variable cost per meal	Fixed cost per meal	Total cost per meal	Net profit or loss	per meal
4000	1.50	0.80	0.75	1.55	− 0.05	(- 5p) (-lp)
4200	1.50	0.80	0.71	1.51	− 0.01	(2p)
4400	1.50	0.80	0.68	1.48	+ 0.02	(<5p)
4600	1.50	0.80	0.63	1.43	+ 0.05	(7p)
4800	1.50	0.80	0.63	1.43	+ 0.07	(10p)
5000	1.50	0.80	0.60	1.40	+ 0.10	

Note: Fixed costs have been worked out to the nearest paisa. Minus sign shows loss, plus sign indicates profit.

Concept of Contribution and Break-Even

'Contribution' refers to the balance remaining after subtracting the variable costs from sales revenue. It would there be expressed as:

Sales Revenue—Variable Costs = Contribution

The concept of contribution therefore represents the amount of money that an establishment earns for covering its fixed costs and net profit margins. Certain establishments who cater to the needs of governmental or social organizations work on a target sales figure, which just covers variable costs and fixed expenses, without making any net profit. In such cases the 'contribution' would be equal to fixed costs.

In such a situation the establishment is said to 'break-even', that is, it makes no profit or loss.

The contribution when calculated as a percentage of sales varies with the cost structure of different establishments. In food service establishments, the fixed costs are higher, and when, due to certain conditions the variable costs rise, as when expensive out of season foods are used, or when the number of customers increases, the contribution decreases because the fixed cost per cover or unit decreases.

The concept of 'contribution' can thus be seen as that part of sales revenue, which can be controlled, because any surpluses earned are, affected by the extent to which control is exercised. The application of these concepts is dealt with in detail when discussing food and other cost controls.

Eight

Cost Control

Food Cost Control

Control is a process by which managers attempt to direct, regulate and restrain the actions of people in order to achieve goals. This is essential in the area of food and other costs because of the many ways in which loss is possible at each stage in a catering operation.

Control may be exercised in many ways, through selection of techniques and devices suitable for each establishment. The techniques available to a manager are establishing standards and procedures, setting examples, observing and correcting employee actions, preparing performance records, reports and budgets.

Two of the main causes of excessive costs in an establishment are inefficiency and waste. The process by which costs are regulated and excessive expenditure guarded against is known as 'cost control'. It is a continuous process at every stage of the catering cycle.

The food costs in any catering establishment whatever its size vary between 40-60 per cent of total sales, depending on the nature of the organization. These costs being variable need to be controlled because on them will depend the amount of profit that the establishment makes.

Besides the variability in costs due to different prices and quantities purchased and used, food is subject to losses in many different ways as it passes through the production and service cycle. The diligent control of these losses therefore, means control of money lost, and hence determines the viability of the food service organisation.

In order to appreciate the methods used in controlling costs in any venture, it would help to enumerate the factors responsible for the leakage of profits in this area. Keeping in mind the sequence in which food is handled in the production cycle and served, these factors are discussed below.

Factors Responsible For Losses

Lack of Proper Supervision at the Point of Receiving Food from Suppliers

At this stage money can be lost through a number of channels.

(i) Improper weights of commodities especially those which are loosely packed, or perishable such as fruits, vegetables, meats, etc. Cereals and pulses in bags not checked for holes in them can also affect weights.

(ii) Improper weighing equipment at the delivery point can affect the weights of foods received, the mistake being made in the recording of the weights. Any extra weight recorded would push up the price of each portion obtained from the food and vice versa.

(iii) Variable quality of foods received: The quality of a food directly affects the number of portions obtained from a standard weight of the item. For example, apples of different sizes with blemishes or irregular surfaces can

123

lead to loss of a lot of money through excessive peelings, trimmings, and so on. Similarly, vegetables like cauliflower with a larger proportion of stem give fewer portions on the plate and therefore cost more per portion. Also cereals, pulses, legumes, etc. if adulterated with inedible material, or packed without cleaning can lead to losses in portion sizes.

(iv) Pilferage at delivery point: At this stage it is much easier to pilfer without actually taking out the food from the establishment. Cases have been known in which the supplier directly delivers to the staff outside the establishment, while the invoices are routinely recorded in the book of the establishment. On checking, the numbers of packs received are in order, but perhaps each one slightly lighter than they should be. Minor differences in weights are generally undetected by an observer, especially when very large quantities are delivered.

(v) *Inaccurate ordering* leading to longer storage time and losses through drying and spoilage.

(vi) *Overcharging* by suppliers or clerical errors.

Inefficient Menu Planning

Unplanned or poorly planned menus for customer requirements can cause unnecessary wastage of ingredients, and thereby push up food costs subsequently lowering profit margins. This can happen when:

(i) Menus are planned without the use of standard yield recipes. They can be financially disastrous, because the numbers of portions obtained are not predictable each time a dish is prepared.

(ii) The menu planners own tastes rather than those of the customers are projected on the menus that end up with dishes unsold.

(iii)   Portion numbers for each dish on the menu are improperly forecasted. They can lead to one dish being completely sold out in the middle of service time while others remain unsold.

(iv)   There is an imbalance of high and low priced dishes on the menu, food costs increase lowering the margin of profit.

(v)   There is little or no flexibility in menu plans to incorporate leftover foods, food costs increase unnecessarily.

(vi)   An item is used for a dish for which it was not meant originally it can push up food costs. For example, an expensive cut of meat used for mince; or a dessert fruit used in fruit salads or for cooked desserts.

(vii)   Dishes are placed on the menu only because the staff can easily prepare them, without attention to quality or customer choice and acceptability.

Kitchen Production

The tools, equipment and techniques used in the cutting, trimming and cooking of food can make or break the establishment in terms of profitability. Losses in this area need far greater control than any others because they can occur in not so obvious ways like:

(a)   Poor peeling or trimming, affecting the number of portions obtained for a unit purchase of food.

(b)   The suitability of cutting and chopping vegetables or meat for each dish will affect the volume of the prepared dish, and hence its selling price. For example, cutting vegetables too finely when large pieces would be just as effective for its presentation, would reduce the volume of the prepared dish, unnecessarily reducing the number of portions for service.

(c)   Using improper cooking methods leading to excessive weight losses and reduced selling portions.

(d) The art of garnishing completed dishes to make them attractive to the customer means recovering cost quicker through more sales. A very tasty dish presented in a sloppy manner can put off customers quite easily.

(e) Picking of food, or excessive indulgence on the pretext of tasting it, before dishing out for service can be a major cause for increasing food costs. If all the staff handling food started picking every testable ingredient at all stages of production, it is not hard to imagine the effect on the consumer and the cash box.

Service of Prepared Food

Food costs can increase in this area through:

(i) Improper availability of portioning equipment.

(ii) Lack of training in portioning correctly at the service point.

(iii) Inefficient temperature control in holding equipment leading to unnecessary losses in portions through the evaporation of moisture, and through shrinkage.

(iv) Picking of finger foods and pilferage when service is slack.

(v) Method of service also affects the portions on the customer's plate, and also the loss in spoilage while serving. For example, in a self-service kitchen, not manned by kitchen staff, disproportionate amounts may be self-served by people who are charged a flat rate for meals. There may be spillage because of lack of practice in serving, by the customers. Some may be very hungry, and hasty while serving themselves. Money lost through plate wastage is also more in a buffet type service, where the charge is fixed. In services where everything served is specifically charged for, the cost control is better.

Cleanring Up

Foods can be lost if clearing up methods are not planned properly. Food from serving dishes not used up completely can be utilized for service to staff and must never be discarded along with plate waste. This can only be done if completely separate sets of people clear service dishes.

Having outlined the areas through which food costs can increase, it becomes easier to formulate a system for their control and increase profit margins. A food cost control system basically requires the use of standard recipes; purchase specifications (drawn up for each item of purchase bought and served); operating policies and procedures which help to control the above mentioned losses at every stage of handling; preparation and service. Policies governing customer and cash control and security also play an important role in controlling costs.

Methods of Controlling Food Costs

(a) Ordering perishable foods in quantities for immediate use in preparation and service.

(b) Ordering semi or non-perishables in quantities that can be turned over fast enough to prevent spoilage.

(c) Close supervision and regular checks at strategic points in the catering cycle.

(d) Using modular equipment for storage, preparation and service, so that portions are not lost in transferring food from one piece of equipment to another.

(e) Portioning in the kitchen and recording the number of portions before sending them for service, and then recording the numbers that are returned to the kitchen.

(f) Offering incentive scheme to staff, for achieving sales targets at established gross profit margins.

(g) Developing lists of customer's favourites through kitchen, service and sales analysis. Then utilizing these to plan imaginative and profitable menus.

(h) Forecasting the quantities of each menu item that will sell so that excess leftovers are avoided,

(i) Developing staff initiative and creativity by inviting their participation in forecasting and planning activities.

(j) Investing on equipment, which will save time of staff on routine jobs so that they can use their initiative better in meal production and food presentation.

(k) Using standardized simple recipes from which portions can be clearly identified.

(l) Substituting low cost ingredients for those that are very expensive, out of stock, or rarely used.

(m) Maintaining control accounts to enable periodic assessments of profitability and efficiency. Such assessments help to pinpoint areas at variance with expected results, so that corrective action can be taken in time.

Table 8.1: Kitchen Analysis Sheet

| Food | Proportion of total food cost | | | |
| | Week I | | Week II | |
	Rs.	%	Rs.	%
Meat	350	14.0	410	13.7
Poultry	200	8.0	230	7.7
Fish	110	4.4	130	4.3
Fruit and Vegetables	280	11.2	400	13.3
Grocery	450	18.0	530	17.7
Provisions	480	19.2	570	19.0
Bread, Flour, etc.	180	7.2	210	7.0
Milk and Cream	250	10.0	290	9.7
Eggs	140	5.6	160	5.3
Sundries	60	2.4	70	2.3
Total	2500	100	3000	100

Note: The percentage of all foods consumed are slightly less in week II as compared to week I, except fruits and vegetables.

The reasons for this can be looked into, and corrective action taken.

Calculations and Cost Statements

In order to ascertain the efficiency of a food service certain calculations are necessary to establish the proportion of costs incurred on various activities in the establishment. Forecasting can be done using a simple calculation with a 'percentage index', which helps to forecast menu items to be prepared for a meal period or a day. The forecast is based on the previous day or week's sales records that should be maintained accurately. The calculation is done in two steps:

(i) $\text{Percentage Index} = \dfrac{\text{Total no. of Item sold}}{\text{Total of all items sold}} \times 100$

(ii) $As) = \dfrac{\text{Percentage index of A} \times \text{Forecast of Total customers}}{100}$

Where $As)$ is the numbers of item A that is forecasted for sale.

Thus the practice of expressing all kitchen costs as percentages of sales helps in making comparisons with figures of previous periods and also set new targets for sales. It also focuses attention on any deviations from targets in particular areas of activity, which can be adjusted to achieve expected results at the end of an accounting period. The costs involved in catering are:

(i)   Food costs
(ii) Labour costs
(iii) Overhead costs

For any operation to succeed all these costs need to be paid for by the cash received from sales. In addition, sales must cover the profit expected from a business whatever the target may be.

All calculations are therefore based on certain ratios developed to measure profitability.

Gross Profit Ratio

Gross profit is the figure that represents the sum total of labour costs, overhead expenses and the net profit of the establishment. When this figure is expressed as a ratio of sales it is known as the gross profit ratio.

If the figure is expressed as a percentage of sales it is referred to as gross profit percentage. Calculation of gross profit, therefore, is simply a matter of subtracting the food costs from the total sales a follows:

$$Gross\ Profit = Total\ sales - Food\ cost$$

The proportions of the various costs differ with the nature of each establishment, the approximate percentages being as shown in Table.

Table 8.2: The proportion of food costs expressed as a percentage of sales for different types of food services

Establishment	Food cost %	Gross profit %
Profit oriented	38-40	60-62
Semi-profit oriented	40-50	50-60
Non-profit oriented	50-60	40-50

Food Cost Ratio

This is also referred to as the kitchen percentage and is calculated by the simple formula: *Food cost Ratio = Food cost/Selling price × 100* If the food cost is known and the target for the kitchen percentage is set, then the selling price can easily be worked out using the above formula.

It is essential for every establishment to make a profit at the end of an accounting period because all costs both fixed and variable need to be covered by the cash received from sales. The amount that remains after subtracting the variable costs would then be the 'contribution' made towards fixed costs of the establishment. It is evident therefore; that even in the so-called non-profit making organizations a minimum profit margin is necessary to contribute towards or cover fixed costs of an operation.

Profit margins may therefore vary according to the goals of an establishment. A governmental organization for the handicapped may make a profit of 2-5 per cent depending on the social costs government and voluntary agencies are prepared to incur. University, college and school, residences or hostels may aim at 5-8 per cent, while profit-making commercial organizations may even go up to a net profit figure of 15 per cent.

Break-even and Contribution

Establishments whose sales figures just cover their variable and fixed costs are said to 'break-even'. Thus they may be classed as non-profit organizations. In other words, when the net profit or loss is zero, the contribution made by the organization just covers the fixed costs. There is a thin dividing line between profit, break-even point and loss, about 1 per cent between profit and loss. It is therefore not practical to expect a food service to operate exactly at the break-even point. The concept of a non-profit business is totally a method of organizing the finances. Under tax laws, the finances can be organized to show a non-profit result, so that no income tax is payable. Every establishment therefore plans for some project to avoid loss. Break-even point in terms of the number of covers may be calculated using the formula given below:

In terms of quality

BEP = Fixed Cost/Contribution per cover

Contribution per cover can be calculated by subtracting variable per cover from average spending power (ASP)

In terms of volume

BEP = Fixed Cost × Selling Price/contribution per unit

Contribution per unit can be calculated by subtracting variable cost per unit from selling price.

Contribution therefore as a percentage of sales, depends on the cost structure of the business. Catering being labour intensive the fixed costs is generally higher than variable costs. When variable costs become high e.g. when certain foods used are out of season or the customers increase, the fixed costs per cover decrease, bringing down the contribution per cover too. The effect of price fluctuations on the contribution to fixed costs and net profit, assuming that the sales in a day amount to Rs. 1,000 in a coffee shop where variable costs are Rs. 400 and the contribution is Rs. 600.

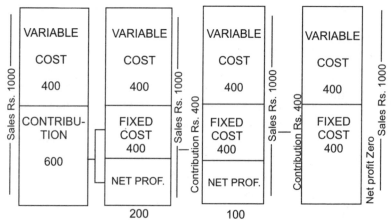

Break-even point may also be calculated for any food service operation, if the kitchen analysis sheets are maintained and the fixed costs calculated accurately.

Examples

A catering establishment budgeted for total sales revenue of Rs. 50,000 for the current year. The labour and overheads were estimated at Rs. 24,000, while the figures for gross profit margins (contribution) in relation to sales mix were:

Menu Item	% Sales Mix	% Gross Profit
Soup	20	60
Meat, fish, poultry	40	40
Vegetables	20	50
Sweets	10	60
Hot beverages	10	60

At the end of the year the sales were achieved, but there was a reduction in the labour and overhead costs by Rs. 1,000. Also the actual gross profit margins and sales mix percentages achieved were as follows:

Menu Item	% Sale	% Gross profit
Soup	20	65
Meat, fish, poultry	30	40
Vegetables	10	60
Sweets	20	60
Hot beverages	20	60

Prepare operating statements to show the effect of change in sales mix on net profit.

Budgeted Operating Statement for year

Item	% Sales mix	Sales (Rs.)	%Gross profit	Gross Profit (Rs.)
Soups	20	10000	60	6000
Met, Fish Poultry	40	20000	40	8000
Vegetables	20	10000	50	5000
Sweets	10	5000	60	3000
Hot beverage	10	5000	60	3000
Total	100	50000	50	25000

Actual Results for year

Menu item	% Sales mix	Sales (Rs.)	% Gross profit	Gross (Rs.)
Soups	20	10000	65	6500
Meat, fish, poultry	30	15000	40	6000
Vegetables	10	5000	60	3000
Sweets	20	10000	60	6000
Hot Beverages	20	10000	60	6000
Total	100	50000	55	275.00
		Less labour and overheads		2,300
		Actual Net Profit Rs.		4,500

It is evident from the above statements that when the sales mix changes it has an effect on the net profit achieved at the end of an accounting period. In the above example, the sales mix percentage for meat, fish and poultry was reduced in favour of sweets and hot beverages, which could have accounted for the reduction in labour cost. Also the food costs actually have been reduced since meat, etc. are expensive items.

The extent of contribution that a particular dish makes to fixed costs and profits is a guide to establish the most profitable sales mix in a menu. The item with the highest contribution is the most profitable. Hence, it is possible to construct menus evolve a sales mix which will give the maximum contribution to fixed costs and net profit. Managers can thus control costs by keeping less quantities of non-profitable items and more of the profitable items on their production schedule.

It is evident from the above discussions that food cost control is vital to the profitability of any catering establishment. In addition, any decisions to close down an establishment during off seasons as in the case of small cafes in summer resorts can be made by an analysis of kitchen percentages and calculations of contributions or profit volume ratios. It is relevant to state here, that any contribution from sales even when the sales volume decreases during off seasons, is paying towards fixed costs and overheads, and unless the establishment is running at a loss on an average, over the year, some contribution is better than none at all.

Costing of Dishes, Meals and Events

Dish Costing

There is no doubt that the exact cost of a dish must be known before it can be served to the customer at a profitable price. Also in non-profit making institutions it is important to cost dishes and meals, accurately to ensure that they are cost effective and cover all costs incurred in their preparation and service therefore the usual practice in catering to determine the total cost of materials used in producing a of a standard quality, and then adding to it a certain percentage or supplement to cover labour and ova costs to arrive at the selling price. This supplement is often as high as 60 per cent; so it is helpful calculate all costs of food accurately and preferably to the third decimal place (Rs. 0.052).

The method of costing dishes is known as 'standard dish costing'. This method is also useful in setting the target) price and usage of the materials, thus helping to detect differences that may occur in the process of i production and service. Once the variations are identified, they can be analysed and the reasons for their occurrence found out and consequently corrected.

Dish costing, however, needs to be checked and altered periodically when food prices change, to mi sure that the values being used in calculations for prices, costs and usages are up-to-date. A sample standard costing sheet.

Stand Costing Sheet

DISH.. ....Soya Chappati   Date....:.......
PORTIONS.......4 (8 Chappatis)

Ingredients	Qty. (g)	Price Rs./kg.	Cost (Rs.)
Whole wheat flour (atta)	75	6.00	0.449
Soya flour	25	8.00	0.200
Rice flour	25	8.00	0.040
Salt	2	2.50	0.050
Fat	10	40.00	0.480
	Total Food Cost (4 portions)		1.219
	Food cost per portion		0.304
	Gross profit %		66%
	Selling price per portion		0.76
	(0.304×100) 76 paise		40

Sample Costing Sheet for Soya Chappati

Costing sheets for each dish on the menu may be filed and recorded for later use as a ready reference for pricing. It is preferable to write the figures in pencil, so that they can be easily erased when there is a change in the price of any ingredient. Costing sheets must be updated regularly once a month or quarterly depending on the variability in prices of ingredients used. Whenever the prices are altered on an existing costing sheet, the selling price must also be calculated again.

A common error made is to calculate the gross profit using the new food cost and increase the worked out selling price by the amount of reduction in the gross profit.

Since percentages are proportions of sales or selling price and not absolute numbers, all the calculations require to be done afresh when food prices change. If food costs remain the same but overheads increase, then also selling prices have to be recalculated to cover them.

The food cost percent of any item can be lowered by raising the price charged on the menu, lowering the amount paid for food and other ingredients, by buying poorer quality or making portions smaller.

However, lowering the quality of the main ingredient, or reducing the size of portions may depress the sales of the item considerably, so one has to be careful in such decisions. Costs are important, but not more important than the customer who pays for them.

Meal or Menu Costing

While calculations similar to those for dish costing would normally establish the selling price of menus, other factors also needs to be considered that will help to sell those menus at the calculated price. These are competitor's prices, policy decisions regarding promotion of new ideas or products, founding up exact calculations of selling prices, which may not always give the estimated gross profit percentage desired. Sometimes, the use of convenience foods in food preparation result in decreased labour and overheads but increase in food cost, so logically less gross profit percentage is required. However, prices are fixed according to what the customer would be willing to pay, and therefore different items on the meal menu would give different profit percentages. For meal costing it helps to prepare costing sheets for individual courses, and then adding up the total costs from the dish costing statements or sheets. By this method flexibility can be built into set menus as well, when another of the same cost can easily substitute a dish, without disturbing the selling price of the meal or the estimated gross profit percentage or functions like a children's party, or a conference lunch, it has been suggested that the charge to the customer should be at least twice the food cost.

The margin being expected to cover the costs of decoration, linen, extra cleaning resulting in higher labour costs, detergent costs, and so on. In certain cases the change may be two and a half or three times depending on the requirements of the occasion. The following examples show the costs and profits obtained by doubling the food cost and fixing the charge.

Variance Analysis

While the standard recipe and the standard dish costing sheet lays the targets for profit margins to be achieved if they are followed meticulously and calculated accurately, in practice this is not so. Differences occur because of price fluctuations or changes in the amounts of ingredients actually used, due to differences in weighing and measuring equipment, and methods which different people use in an establishment. These differences are known as 'variances' and may be either adverse or favourable in terms of the effects on the profits of the establishment. Variances are generally written as 'A' or 'T' standing for adverse or favourable as the case may be.

The variance has resulted from two elements the increase in price, and the quantity of ingredients used. The contribution of each element to the total variance can be calculated by using the following formula

(i) Price variance = Actual price – Standard price × Actual quantity

(ii) Material usage variance = Actual quantity – Standard quantity × Standard price

If an adverse variance were identified in any of the elements mentioned above, its effect would be a reduction in profits. If the variance were favourable, the effect would be an increase in profits.

Labour Cost Control

Since catering is a service industry, labour or staff costs form the largest expense next to food. Labour costs include salaries of staff and the value of all benefits provided to them, such as meals, medical facilities, housing, insurance, bonus, pension and uniforms. Controlling labour cost therefore involves control of expenses in all the areas listed, which is difficult because of the relatively fixed nature of the costs.

Meals

According to the policy of the establishment, a subsidy is generally given for staff meals, and therefore not subject to change in the short run unless the policy changes. The subsidy is worked out on the basis of average costs.

For determining the cost of employee's meals therefore, the numbers of meals served are multiplied by the estimated average cost per meal. Then the cost of three meals is added together to arrive at the cost of employee's meals per day. For example, if 20 breakfasts are consumed at Rs. 2 each, 30 lunches at Rs. 3 each and 20 dinners at Rs. 4 each. Then the cost of meals per day can be easily calculated. The differences in the numbers eating the different meals is due to work scheduling, and are thus taken care of in the calculation of daily meal costs.

Management can control employee meal costs by fixing the subsidy on meals, and issuing coupon book for a week. The employee at the same menu price pays anything eaten by employees beyond the coupon values for as the customers.

Bonus

The payment of bonuses in directly related to productivity and therefore profits. Establishments will like to be able to pay bonus to staff, as they will earn it only in proportion to sales revenues earned. Management control on bonus payments is limited as staff unions negotiate it.

1. *Nature of the business:* Whether traditional or fast food. If a traditional waiter service is changed to a fast food one labour cost decreases.

2. *Volume of business* i.e. the proportion of personnel employed to volume of customers. Determine the minimum staff necessary even if business is low, and ensure that they are fully utilized.

3. *Peak Periods:* Look at time of the day when maximum customers arrive or the days of the week schedule employees according to weekly forecasts.

Uniforms

The Cost of uniforms to an establishment varies with its policy. Where employees are paid uniform allowances the costs can be easily determined, but where establishments take on the responsibility of providing uniforms, the costs of laundry are also usually borne by the establishment with the latter policy on uniforms.

Some establishments may fix prices of meals for employees at lower (discounted), values without paying out a monetary subsidy to employees. The accounts section can account for their meals separately. Other establishments may have separately cooked employee meals as a set menu, which is served in an employees canteen, whether they eat all of it or not. Here also the employees' meals can be costed easily.

Medical Facilities

Every establishment has to provide medical facilities for their staff. Some may provide the facilities or reimburse the costs to employees when they need medical attention.

The surest way to control costs in this area is to ensure that employees remain in good health. This can be done by providing a healthy work environment, social hours of work, limiting hours to ensure that fatigue exhaustion does not set in, and providing nutritious meals at work.

Housing

Housing costs are generally costs as fixed subsidies (usually 10 per cent of house rent with maximum limit) as for meals. These vary slightly according to availability of accommodation that staffs themselves find. In smaller establishments no housing is provided and the one or two workers may sleep on the premises for security reasons. Thus the control of housing costs is much more difficult, except by fixing a ceiling.

Insurance and Pension

These costs are relatively fixed and worked out on the basis of salaries. The area of control is therefore limited.

1. *Function and seasonal catering*: Whether customer's demands change with the seasons. If there are too many functions how best to schedule staff to prevent additional part-timer from being used.
2. There are uses of labour and time saving devices such as:
   (i)   Conveyors for moving goods, vertical and horizontal cutters, slicers, dicers and shredders to replace knife work.
   (ii) Liquid dispensers to speed up beverage service and save time on portioning and handling,
   (iii) Electric ovens
   (iv) Convenience foods
3. *Layout of stores and kitchen*: If layout is poor more staff will be required and labour costs increase. Certain concrete steps can be taken to control labour cost, after a total appraisal of the establishment has been made. Some suggestions are:
   (i) Schedule staff on shift basis, so that they arrive only when needed.
   (ii) Staff should report to work in uniform and not change after reporting.
   (iii) Some part-time staff should be maintained on a regular

basis with fewer full-time permanent employees. Such employees can be available on call and paid on hourly or daily basis,

(iv) Use of the overtime is dependent on the union contract situation, but should be limited as far as possible. It is however cheaper to pay overtime to a regular employee, than hire untrained outside staff. But overtime should be planned and prearranged, so that staff does not misuse the facility by slowing down during working hours everyday.

(v) Send personnel home early if they have no work on particular days. This idea however, works well only with service personnel, but there has to be a union agreement on paying them less when there is no work. For example union policy may be that every employee gets a minimum of four hours pay if he reports on duty. Tips are important for high standards of service but may also act adversely when customer numbers drop.

The only real way to save labour costs is to retain staff once they join an staff once they join an establishment, so that costs of turnover are avoided. To be able to do this it is important to be aware of the costs of turnover. Every time an employee leaves a new one has to be recruited and costs are incurred on stationary, interview time, communications, initial low productivity, supervision, badges, uniforms, brochures on policy and procedures. time and materials for physical and medical examinations.

Although a certain amount of employee turnover is expected, because of temporary workers in the industry and retirement, much of the permanent employee turnover should be avoided. Turnover does bring fresh ideas into the food service but permanence of employees to implement ideas is essential too, for success.

Some manager thinks that an unfilled vacancy is labour cost saved. This is not a good idea because overtime efficiency falls. If a very good employee leaves, a manager may have to hire two instead which will increase costs. It is good policy to plan increase in salary on a regular basis and try and retain good staff.

Overhead Cost Control

Overheads include all cost, which cannot directly be identified with food products. These included rent, rates depreciation, fuel, cleaning materials, administrative and selling costs. Of these costs some are controllable and some are beyond control or uncontrollable identifies the two categories of overhead costs.

Controllable Cost	Non-Controllable Cost
. Heat, Light, Power, Gas	Interest
. Stationary, Disposable plants, Cups etc.	Depreciation
. Glass. China, Silver Insurance	Insurance
. Line, laundry, uniform	Taxes (real estate and income tax)
	Rent
. Cleaning	
. Security	
. Advertising	
. Donations	

From it is apparent that there are a lot more overhead cost which a manager can control. Each of these costs is discussed below.

Heat, Light, and Power and Gas

The resources constitute the energy resources of the establishment, and methods of controlling them have been discussed. Human efforts however, which is also an important early source, the use of which requires optimisation by proper work scheduling is not an overhead cost and therefore discussed under labour cost.

143

Stationary

May food services use unnecessary paper supplies and stationary? This can easily be controlled by the use of appropriate equipment. Examples are installation of electronic cash register, which help to do away with duplicate and triplicate vouchers, register for sales records etc. Similarly the use of paper napkin dispensers and electronic hand driers can prevent wastage of serviettes and paper towels. Doubtless, the initial equipment cost will increase but in the long run they would fully by control of stationary use initial equipment cost will increase but in the long run they would fall by control of stationary use.

Disposables

Expenses on disposable supplies such as plates, cup and napkins can also be curtailed by the use of, Besides the cost of disposable supplies and stationary, getting rid of large amounts of used paper and supplies creates additional work for staff.

Glass, China, Silver

Glass and China costs in any establishment only increase because of breakage. While costs on silver are generally due to carelessness ill intentions of staff. Cutlery is often pilfered or unintentionally thrown into garbage along with plate waste. Since these are expensive items subject to constant use, expenses on them may be curtailed by the installation of a dish washing machine. Glass is more vulnerable, to breakage than china, and can be preserved by such installations. If however, a dies washing machine is not affordable, and the nature and volume of the business does not demand one, then only a glass washing machine may be installed. As far as silver is concerned better supervision during meal times and a total account of the silver after it is washed at the end of every meal, may be routinely done.

This not only helps to pin-point the careless staff, but locates any lost silver by searching for it on the spot. This practice also installs in staff a sense of responsibility and caution particularly if the duty of counting is assigned to service staff in rotation every week.

Line, Laundry, Uniforms

The only way to control expenses on line and uniforms and therefore laundry costs is to distribute line to staff who are responsible for their washing and care. If the establishment is large and adopts a waiter service, laundry service staff removes all fresh napkins from a table which are not required during service. For example, when a table is laid four customers and only three people arrive to use that table the fourth place setting including napkin and silver may be removed before the customers are served.

Another alternative is to replace linen by easy clean tablemats or disposable mats. The cost effectiveness may be determined along with other effects like atmosphere; decor etc., when taking decisions pertaining to service areas. This is because while cost savings are important, customer's expectations take higher priority. It is not worth saving on laundry at the cost of even on customer.

Cleaning

While cleanliness is of utmost importance in any food service, it must be remembered that the amount of detergent used for various typing of cleaning, is not as important the right type of detergent in the right quantities. An effective detergent is required only in small quantities to do a good cleaning job.

Cleaning costs can therefore be controlled best by proper training of staff in the right quantities of a detergent to use, and by close supervision. Unfortunately this is an area, which is least supervised in any establishment, without realising that along with extra detergents, lot of money is literally thrown down the drain.

It is also more economical to use as few varieties of detergents in an establishment as possible.

Regular cleaning and maintenance of silver, floors, walls and work surfaces will require less cleaning materials and effort than cleaning occasionally.

Security

The general feeling of most managers is that anything spent on security is not a waste of money. But there must still be a limit. When expenses on security start digging into the profitability of an establishment, it is time to control expenses on security and make the food service more secure.

In small establishments one uniformed armed security man around the clock may be enough to deter people from attempting to steal establishment resource. To get reliable security men is also not difficult these days because there are security agencies who supply staff on contractual basis. It is the total responsibility of the agency to see that someone is posted with the establishment all the time. For most catering staff a security check at the exit and a uniform is enough deterrent against theft. But against outside intruders a single man may be helpless. So expenditure incurred on an alarm system is well worth the cost.

A variety of systems are marketed and the choice will have to be left to the management decide which is the most suitable for each establishment, according to its size.

Advertising

The best mode of advertising for any food service, 'whatever its size, is word of mount' and the cost is high quality food and service at all times. Therefore the actual advertising costs nothing. If a food service is spending on advertising it need to divert the expenditure on improving the quality of its products, food and service. Once this is done the costs on advertising will be automatically get controlled.

Donations

Donations given by any business for social causes are from accounting point of view an expense but in effect. They bring about a cost saving, because such expenses are exempt from income tax payments.

Donations therefore help to organise the profits to the establishment. Besides these donations are the cheapest way of advertising the food service.

If a manager can control and bring down even some of the above costs in his establishment, his operative profits. Will rise immediately.

A good cost control system is based on an understanding of behaviour of food and other costs in relation to the volume of sales; changes in selling prices or menu composition; and the extent to which changes in technology can effect cost structures of the establishment. Equipment with this understanding, and that of human behaviour (staff and customers), it is possible to predict the impact of a decision, before it is implemented, and thereby control costs, sales and profits effectively.

Nine

Pricing

The process of determining what to charge the customer for door items, menus or services, may be termed as 'pricing'. In commercial catering, prices depend a great because the proportion of fixed costs is relatively high and the profit margins expected are far greater than those for social institutions. The latter include hostels, lunchrooms, homes for the handicapped, and so on. In these, pricing takes on a cost-effective rather than a profit-making goal.

As discussed earlier, there is a definite relationship between the price level and the volume of sales, High prices are almost always accompanied by a low volume of sales. In food service establishments, however, the volume of sales is the most important determinant of profitability. Therefore, if the right price levels are not arrived at, the desired volume of sales cannot be achieved. Thus, the pricing policy is the most critical factor in the assessment of the viability of an establishment: more so, when there is increasing competition in the field of food service.

Future, technological changes have altered the existing cost structures by shifting the emphasis from one type of cost to another. For instance, where certain jobs are totally or partially mechanized, the labour costs incurred previously have shifted to capital costs. This shift has its effects on the methods of determining prices.

Methods of Pricing

The two methods of pricing commonly used are: (a) Cost plus methods, and (b) Rate of return method.

Cost Plus Pricing

This method involves the calculation of the food cost per unit of sales for details) and then a given percentage of gross profit is added to the value to arrive at the selling price per unit. This percentage is intended to cover the cost of labour and overhead expenses while also leaving a margin of net profit. The net profit percentage required will depend on the pricing policy of the particular establishment. Food operations generally add 150 per cent to food cost.

(a) Cost plus pricing is based on cost, and does not take into account the demand for the product or service. Its indiscriminate use, therefore, becomes irrational.
(b) Net profit becomes the direct function of sales turnover.
(c) The gross profit margin is added to the food cost and the net profit is unrelated to the capital invested.

The cost-plus method is easy to apply and understand, and is therefore widely used. It has, however, certain disadvantages like.

Rate of Return Pricing

This method is based on the relationship of net profit to capital investment. By this method the likelihood of reaching net profit targets is greater, provided that the estimated sales volume is achieved and the gross profit margins are maintained.

The rate of return method of pricing, however, has some disadvantages:

(a) It is purely profit-oriented and has little scope for flexibility.
(b) Its approach to pricing problems is too simple to be realistic.
(c) It does not generally go by the demands of customer or the market.

At best, the above methods can be useful in evaluating performance, or act as basis guides in pricing.

They are, however, not useful in appraising investments.

Having calculated the profit multiplier (PM) values for all the elements of the sales mix, prices can be reviewed in a number of ways to achieve a net profit increase of 10 per cent. These are:

(i) The menu prices of all items can be increased by 1.25 per cent to achieve a net profit increase of 10 per cent because the total of all PM values is 8.0 (8 ×1.25 = 10).
(ii) If we increase the prices of all meat dishes by 2 per cent, this will increase the net profit by 6.4 per cent (2 × 3.20, i.e. PM). In addition, if the prices of sweets are increased by 3 per cent, the net profit increase will be 3.6 per cent 93 × 1.20). Together this will affect an increase of 10 per cent in the net profit, which is what is desired.

Thus, a number of pricing decisions are feasible by simple calculations using the profit multiplied. It is good pricing management policy to bring about only slight increases in the prices of popular dishes, without generally increasing the prices of all menu items, to achieve the desire results. This helps to achieve the necessary profit margins while still maintaining the goodwill of the customers.

Castos Affecting Pricing

Location of the Food Service :The situation of a food service establishment will affect greatly the prices charged to the customer. It is common experience to find that a coffee shop situated in a market place, where the volume of sales common experience to find that a coffee shop situated in a market place, where the volume of sales exacted is higher, would price products slightly lower than if it was situated in a posh residential area. In the latter, the occasional customer would have to be charged for the higher fixed costs per unit of sales incurred by the establishment. However, location has less importance for a luxury restaurant because people who choose to go to them are usually wiling to travel to enjoy them.

Menu

The composition of the menu determines the pricing because of the direct relationship between food costs and selling prices. When sales are slack cheaper substitute ingredients for dishes helps to reduce food cost without changes in the prices normally charged. This hops to increase the profit margin and offset the impact of lowered sales volume. Similarly, changes in consistency or texture can affect portions served, and consequently the prices charged,. The large the variety offered in the menu, the greater will be the range of prices charged. The limited menu will almost always have a fixed range of prices.

Service Method

The nature of the service offered to customers has its effect on pricing. For instance, if self-service system were followed, the prices would not be rewired to cover the service charge. Besides, the turnover of customers is expected to be faster leading to a greater sales volume, and therefore a lower food cost percentage of sales, and a consequent lower price structure. On the other hand, a traditional waiter service puts up the prices because of the higher staff costs necessary, more space needed to serve and seat the customer, greater amounts of cutlery, amounts of cutlery, crockery and table appointments required, and so on.

Likes And Dislikes of Customers

More often the not people like to eat what they cannot get at home or get in hostel or other institution, and therefore go out for a change. The favourites of different customers can affect the prices depending on the demand created. Some favourites with all children are burgers, pizzas, ice creams, chips, 'tikkis'. Cutlets or 'chat'. Adults would normally prefer a full meal of curry, nana, salad and a sweet.

Purchasing Power as related to the Expectations of Customers

Prices are affected by how much a customer is willing to pay for a particular food item or meal. For instance, irrespective of the food cost of a hamburger to the caterer, a customer is only prepared to pay upto Rs. 4 or Rs. 4.50 for it, while he would pay even Rs. 7 or 89 for an ice-cream. Very often therefore, prices are adjusted to suit the purchasing power or buying capacity of the customer. In such cases profits are not achieved through prices calculated for predetermined percentages, but through increasing the volume of sales.

It is the general impression of managers that customers are very price conscious, and aware of the costs at various food services. They may even go to the extent of fixing low prices for their menus to attract customers others may fix their prices very high, hoping customers will relate the price to quality. Both these attitudes to pricing are unrewarding, because customers are not that interested in the price once they have decided to eat out. People do decide in advance the general price category, which reflects in their choice of the food service to which they go. Further, their choice of menu takes care of their spending limits.

However, the choices are based on a fair idea about the comparative prices of different types of establishments like dhobis, takeaways, cafeterias, coffee shops and luxury restaurants.

Environmental Conditions

Any factors in the environment which have an impact on food costs, labour costs, overhead expenses or sales volume affect pricing. Some such factors are:

(i)   Poor harvest leading to less production of fresh fruits and vegetables, cereals and pulses, legumes, etc. and thereby thither prices of those food items.

(ii)   Sometimes diseases in farm animals can lead to shortage of good meats or make meats more expensive to buy.

(iii)   A transport strike may inhibit transportation of food from growing to manufacturing of food from growing to manufacturing areas and to those of consumption as well, pushing up food costs.

(iv)   Riots leading to curfew conditions can result in a drastic fall in the number of customers affecting the sales.

(v)   Inflationary conditions created by government policies involving extortion of food, or taxation trees encouraging the setting up of more food processing industries would result in a price rise for raw foods.

(vii)   Changes in weather conditions, which keep people indoors, can affect the number of customers in food service establishments.

(viii) Shortages of fuel like electricity, cooking gas, coal, etc. which are so common in developing countries, can be responsible for increasing overhead costs and thereby affecting prices.

(ix)   Strike or "go slow" at work by staff, or cooking gas, coal, etc. which are so common in developing countries an be responsible for increasing overhead costs and thereby affecting prices.

The type of conditions in the environment, both external and internal, can therefore be varied depending on the type of food service establishment, its situation, the country, etc.

Making Pricing Decisions

Pricing decisions are generally made at higher levels of management from where the establishment can be viewed in its total perspective, with an understanding of the impact of different pricing policies on profitability. Pricing decisions are affected by the elasticity of demand, the cost structure of the enterprise and its pricing policy.

The more elastic the demand, the greater is the scope for an imaginative pricing policy. It is for this reason that special discounts, off season rates, or prices for specials on the menu can be offered on special occasion. These are primarily designed to optimise profits through increasing the volume of sales, capturing the mood the customers during festive seasons and so on. Imaginative pricing, however, is only useful over short periods, because the 'price tactics' resorted to are not often good enough to cover variable costs. This is also referred to as 'contribution pricing'. The contribution approach to pricing is based on the fact that in certain situations, it may be better to sell individual products at a price just in excess of variable costs.

This may to help the establishment to break-even, but at least make some contribution to fixed costs, rather than none at all. This type off approach is resorted to in case where there are only seasonal customers, as in hill or tourist resorts in out of the way places which are prone to under-utilised capacity during contain periods. Price discretion rewires skill, initiative, creativity and an accurate judgment of the customers' mood and receptivity to new ideas all these are developed with experience. When the variable costs ware low, as in times of bumper crops: a wider range of prices can be profitably charged, while still offering the customer a wide choice. When the fixed costs of an establishment are high, profit stability decreased, because prices charged have to follow market forces. In such case, the 'cost plus' method of pricing becomes baseless.

All pricing decisions are governed by the policies laid out for particular establishments. These are related to price, costs, demand and profit margins. Pricing has always been a challenge to cater because he deals with a large quality of perishable commodities. It is therefore important to be able to understand the behaviour of all costs, and to predict the impact of changes in them on the profitability of a food service operation.

Today, with catering becoming more and more professional, and the variety of services demanded by the customer ever increasing, an intuitive approach to pricing is not enough. Accurate forecasting and tight controls through constant monitoring are required, so that methods based on sound accounting systems can be developed. It is vital to bear in mind that all calculations of costs, menu prices, and profit margins need to be reviewed from time to time to inculcate changes in cost structures, resulting from fluctuation in variable costs, customer demand, labour problems, time allocation of people due to menu changes or staff problems.

A manager must however, keep in mind that he is not only selling food but a package of service, charm, warmth, atmosphere, cleanliness, location and music all of which affect pricing decisions.

It also becomes clear therefore that management must be devoted to the revenue controlling aspects of the business, as well as to its cost aspects, in proportion to their respective effects on profitability. Without this understanding and the ability to predict the effects of pricing decisions prior to their implementation, a caterer cannot ensure success for his food service.

Ten

Purchasing Equipment

Purchasing is that activity which is directed towards securing materials, supplies and equipment required for the operations of a food service or animation. It represents the act of buying at a price. In the broader sense purchasing is a management actively which involves planning, policy-marking and conducting research and development activities, required for proper selection of materials and sources of materials and sources of purchase: following-up to ensure proper delivery: and inspection for quality. In addition, it covers the coordination of activities of related departments.

Purchasing of equipment involves tapping the proper supply, as the expenditure on equipment form part of the capital investment of the organization. For selecting the right supplier for each type of equipment it is necessary to prepare a list of suppliers and the special equipment items offered by them. The Sources from which such a list can be compiled are:

(i)   Past experience.

(ii)   Interviewing salesmen.

(iii)   Equipment catalogues.

(iv)   Trade directories and journals.

(v)   Competitor's experiences.

(vi) Trade fairs, seminars, conferences and conventions.

(vii) Requests for quotations.

Once the source of supply has been determined the methods used to acquire equipment would be determined by the kind or nature of the equipment in terms of whether it is a special or a general purpose one.

The methods of purchasing equipment differ from methods used for raw materials because equipment is an infrequent nonrecurring item of purchase and each transaction is negotiated separately. It is very rare to find a piece of equipment being recorded because the life of one piece is expected to extend over a span is also because unused pieces in showrooms or stores depreciate faster than equipment in use.

That is why it is important to plan equipment requirements well in advance, as it is not possible to buy them at short notice. The lead-time, that is, the interval between placing the order and actual delivery varies with the notice. The lead-time is greater in the case of custom-built equipment because it has to make to suit specific needs.

Purchase of capital equipment is influences by the number of people in an establishment. If purchasing is part of a modernization programmed for an existing unit it has to be considered by top management long before the actual purchase is initiated. A purchasing decision is the result of a report from the user department, where a need arises for particular equipment. The report is expected to give the reasons for the need; the estimated cost involved it booth, and the expected savings from its use. After the purchases, finance officers, catering managements, and staff operators who would ultimately be directly involved with the operation of the equipment.

The determines the exac 0t size of the unit to be bought in relation to the space available for its location; the equipments in terms of electricity load available in the case of electrical appliances, existing installation and maintenance facilities; production requirements, and so on. For purchasing any equipment it is important to establish clear specifications of what is required. Indicates a sample of a specification for a sink unit:

The specifications for capital equipment are quit flexible because equipment designed by different manufacturing for the same purpose vary in their characteristics. Not all equipment meet one set of specifications, and setting rigid specifications means paying more for it because the competition for the manufacture is reduced. However, all specifications must be clear and cover aspects relating to material, construction size, colour, finish and cost. The idea is to give clear instructions to the manufacture or supplier, of what exactly would be accepted. If a prices does not conform to specification, than the buyer has the right to reject it, a right that he cannot exercise if his specification is vague.

In making purchase decisions for heavy equipment it is not wise to depend too much on engineers because they make very rigid specifications, which may require alteration in existing design and delay the delivery of the unit. Detailed information of all equipment purchased needs to be recorded with respect to its make, item number, date of purchase, expected life, production captivity, source of supply, price, etc. This helps those in charge of operation and maintenance to work out schedules for the upkeep of the equipment. Further, in case there is ever need to order spare parts there is no problem in communicating with the dealers or manufactures. Records also help to identify any changes that may have been introduced in later models, and are a useful aid in case the piece needs to be recorded.

(a) Even though initial investment may be reasonable for quality and usefulness, it is wise to add on the costs of emergency repairs, costs involved in getting hold of qualified engineers for regular maintenance and servicing and costs of communications with outside agencies. Running costs due to lack of acclimatization of units manufactured in advanced countries for the specific purpose due to lack of acclimatization of units manufactured in advanced countries for the purpose of using them in tropical, is a factor often overlook.

(b) This refers to the time period for which the equipment may be in disuse because of delay in getting parts for repairs and eminence.

(c) Another facet of purchasing equipment is the value of the accessories that go with the main unit. Sometimes these 'extra' are equal to the price of the basic equipment. It might be wise to consider buying these from source other than that of the main equipment, because the manufacture may not be manufacturing the accessories himself.

1. Very often suppliers may insist on caking a survey of the conditions under which their product is gaunt to be operated. If this service is not available voluntarily it is wise for the buyer to ask for it, so that the vendor can guarantee its efficiency in use. The survey helps the manufactures to families himself with the types of materials that are going to come in contact with the equipment. He can then judge as to whether his unit is properly designed for the purpose, in terms of functional efficiency. As a result the vendor can often suggest economic use if he knows where and how the unit is going to the positioned, or who is going to use it, and how.

2. This service is generally provided by the manufacturer for heavy catering equipment and is included in the price. The service is sometimes charged separately in which case optional charges are assessed on the basis of actual time and expenses incurred in the installation.

3. This may be provided as part of the installation service. Usually the service engineer supervises the installation and assists in training the operating staff. This is an important feature because vendors frequently include a clause in their warranty agreements, which relives them of the responsibility for damage to the equipment caused by improper operation. If the vendors had trained the operator it is hared for him to avoid his warranty obligation by claiming that operator was incompetent.

4. This includes service during the warranty period, as service after it. On most capital equipment, three is a written guarantee against failure of the equipment for faulty design or defective parts for a period generally extending up to one year, during which attention to the equipment in case of faults developing is given by the manufacture or supplier. After the 'the 'running in' period the buyer is expected to pay for all the services offered which are generally reflected in the price.

Purchase Procedure

The procedure for purchasing involves a number of steps:

(a) The recognition of a need.
(b) Specification of the required item.
(c) Selection of the sources of supply.
(d) Enquires regarding the price.
(e) Placing the order.
(f) Following up the order.
(g) Checking the equipment and invoices received against specification.
(h) Maintaining records and files.
(i) Maintaining public relations with vendors.

Other activities which need attention are, the mode of delivery, receipt of incoming goods, their inspection, store-keeping, inventory control and taking care of scrap and surplus disposals.

Purchasing Methods

There are a number of methods used for buying equipment. For small equipment like kitchen tools, cutlery, table appointments and the like, methods which are quite informal are used, which for larger equipment formal methods are generally employed, all of which are discussed below:

Informal or Open Market Buying

This methods in generally used by small establishments who required purchasing a piece of equipment only once in a while. A survey of the market is made to find out what designs of the needed equipment are available. The prices are checked along with quality and other services offered. The contact between buyer and supplier may be made on telephone followed be the supplier calling on the buyer. Price quotations are obtained informally and the purchasing decision made which best suits the needs of the establishment.

Formal Competitive Bid Buying

In this method specifications of the equipment to be purchased are written out and quotations are invited from sellers, by advertising in dailies or trade journals. Sealed quotations or bids when received are than opened in the presence of the sellers or their representatives, and at last three responsible head of allied placed with the offering supplier.

Competitive bidding can be made a less formal method by simply sending printed requests with specifications only to interested sellers. This reduces the administrative work a great deal and the item can be purchased in much shorter time unless it needs to be manufactured specially to suit the individual needs of an establishment. While an order is expected to be placed with the lowest bidder, this is not always done unless quality conditions are met.

All bids are expected to state the date, method of delivery, terms of payment, willingness to accept part or all of the bid, any discounts or other terms of negotiation and date of closing of bids.

Negotiated Buying

This is semiformal method used only when an item is restricted in its availability and therefore limited in supply. The method is flexible and enables buyers to make purchasing decisions fast enough to benefit from a fluctuating market. The buyers contact sellers and request them to submit bids in writing. The buyers are less strict in their procedures for acceptance, them in the competitive bid method.

Auction Buying

This method is only suitable for establishments which can make on the spot purchasing decisions because in involves offering sport bids for an item in a situation where there are a number of bidders but no formal contract. Selling is generally on an "as is where is" basis with no responsibility or guarantee offered by the seller and the payment is made generally in cash, which is paid on the spot.

This method of purchasing is sometimes useful, if one wishes to buy used equipment or an outdated model, which may serve the needs of a particular establishment. This method of purchasing can provide good bargains sometimes, because of the urgency of the seller to dispense with the equipment. The advantages to the buyer are in terms of initial low price, immediate delivery and ability to inspect the equipment before purchasing, which is not always the case with new equipment especially larger units that are generally manufactured on order.

Blanket Order Purchasing

This is a good method to use when buying single not too expensive fixed price items such as crockery, cutlery, dishes, small kitchen equipment like knives, ladles, etc. It involves an agreement with the supplier to provide a certain quality of specified items for a period of times at an agreed price. If for some reason the price cannot be specified, a method of calculating it is built into the contract. The deliveries are then made at contract periods, under what is known as a specified 'release' system.

A second type of blanket order involves an agreement to supply all the buyer's needs for certain items for specified time like a year. In such a method the quality of the order is not predetermined and cannot be known until the time of the contract is over.

The advantage of 'blanket order' purchasing is that a variety of items can be purchased from one supplier and deliveries are frequent an on time because the supplier is sure of his commitment. It also involves less paper work every time a request is to be made for any item, as the description of the item covered in the lists contracted for are a guide to both buyers and sellers. Also it is possible to buy at lower prices because of the possibility of getting quantity discounts by grouping items required.

In blanket order purchasing the prices can be handled in one of three way:

(a) By negotiating firm prices for each item, on the list of the supplier.
(b) By specifying the market price and using some standard method of calculating it for every delivery.
(c) By establishing a ceiling price and using the actual prevailing price each time delivery is made.

Consignment Buying or 'Stockless Purchasing'

As the name suggests to buyer does not hold the stock of the items, and so suppliers who are nearest the location of the establishment are preferred. This method is therefore on lay applied for the purchase of those items of equipments which are required frequently but at irregular intervals, such as cutlery, crockery, small kitchen tools, etc.

The buyer is expected to make a list of items along with specifications, and suppliers quote their prices on those lists. The advantage of this method is that the buyer's capital investment on stock is minimized; paper work is reduced and prices and lead-time are reduced. Time and effort on maintaining and issuing stock is transferred to the supplier and storage space is released in the establishment for use of frequently used regular items.

Purchasing Decisions

The need for purchase of any equipment is determined by a number of factors such as:

(i) *The complexity of the food preparation process*: This can be analysed to study the time and effort spent on a particular activity. For example, peeling potatoes, carrots or any hard vegetable is a very time and effort consuming activity, as well as a necessary one in any traditional food service establishment. The purchase of a peeling machine would reduce effort and time, while giving a uniform product in terms of peeled potatoes. It would also make the environment for the activity more hygienic by passing peels to the outside of the kitchen through an outlet attached to the machine.

(ii) *Volume of food cooked*: The will affect decisions regarding the size of equipment needed.

(iii) *The cooking procedure*: If food is cooked in batches then the needs will vary even though a large volume of food may be required through a serving day.

(iv)   *Volume of food cooked*: These are important determinations of equipment needs.

(v)   *The form in which food is purchased*: Raw, convenience, or ready prepared forms will affect equipment needed.

(vi)   *Staffing position*: The number of man-hours and type of skills available will determine what equipment will be required to supplement staff.

(vii) *Space available for installation and use*: The space available is of utmost importance especially in buildings not planned for the use of newer equipment. Also shape of space and point of location is an important a consideration. Which the above enactors are important it is also necessary to work out specifically the present needs of the establishment. Keeping in mind the possibility of future expansion.

Payment for Equipment

Since purchasing equipment involves varying degrees of investment different methods are used for payment. It may be made in instalments, or paid in one lot in advance of delivery or after it, as settled mutually between buyer and seller. In most cases a 25 per cent down payment is required at the time of placing the order to guard the manufacture against orders being cancelled. This also gives him the initial balance for material required to start the manufacture of the unit.

Methods are used for payment. IT may be made in instalments, or paid in one lot in advance of delivery or after it, as settled mutually between buyer and seller. In most cases a 25 per cent down payment is required at the time of placing the order to guard the manufacture against orders being cancelled. This also gees him the initial blasé for material required to start the manufacture of the unit.

Eleven

Food Purchasing

Purchasing good food is the basis for preparing and serving meals that are acceptable to the customer. Unlike purchasing for the home, the food service manager cannot always go to the market and choose what he wants from the variety available. In fact, he has the disadvantage of not being able to actually see the food he is buying till it comes to his door. This makes food purchasing a more difficult but challenging task.

For buying well, the person responsible for placing the orders for food on behalf of his customers must know:

(a) How various commodities are marketed and handled? Food and food products available in markets undergo a constant change. Newer varieties of fresh fruits and vegetables are constantly researched to improve size, colour, texture and flavour. A classic example is the appearance of newer varieties of citrus fruits and mangoes, different sizes of chillies, cabbages, potatoes and so on. Apart from the different forms and varieties grown, fresh food is available in forms as desired by a consumer. For example, meat can be purchased as chops, boneless, leg of mutton for roast, mince, etc. Fish may be bought whole or filleted as required.

Freezing technology has added a number of possibilities to the range available by capturing the freshness and qualities of foods at their different stages of growth and preparation.

Advances in processing technology are responsible for additional varieties of packaged foods made available to consumers. Instant foods have all become familiar to most buyers. In addition, there is a wide range of ingredients offered in the form of syrups, spices, flavouring, food colours, stabilizers and preservatives, to enhance the sensory and keeping qualities of food.

(b) What food and food products are available in the market in particular seasons? The manner in which foods are brought from the farms or factories to the markets provides a good index to their nutritional and keeping qualities. Fresh foods, which have to be, transported long distances reach the consumer after a lapse of a few days. It is therefore good policy to use fresh produce especially meat, fish; poultry and vegetables as soon as they are received in a food service establishment.

Different foods are packed and handled in different ways. For example, radishes and carrots are often packed in jute bags in standard weights and transported while cabbages or cauliflowers may simply be stacked one on top of the other directly in a truck. On their receipt in markets, vendors or retailers sometimes scrape carrots and radishes and wash them in water before arranging them in their stalls or shops for sales. Such handling improves the sheen, colour and smoothness of the vegetables and attracts buyers. But such treatment reduces the keeping qualities. It is therefore important to know what handling procedures are followed before placing orders for foods. Appearances should not be the only characteristic on which to base one's decisions regarding food purchasing. Quality characteristics of different foods must be kept in mind.

(c) Preventing Prices and fluctuations occurring from time to time in wholesale and retail markets:

Prices of foods fluctuate from season to season, and also in response to external to external factors like famines, droughts, factory closures, customer demand, and so on. Knowledge of these equips a food buyer to buy the cheapest and best products if he is vigilant of market conditions. An occasional visit to markets wholesale and retail, is good policy instead of depending entirely on the price quotations and qualities offered by the suppliers. Suppliers tend to offer products, which are most profitable to them within their conditions of supply, and the best quality may never reach an establishment unless the supplier is aware of the buyer's knowledge. Knowing market prices also helps to make use of seasons of glut in terms of buying in quantities, which carry cash discounts.

(d) Size and types of packs available for bulk purchasing:

Foods of the same quality come in may sizes and types of packs. For example, rice may be purchased in gunny bags of 25 kg each or polybags of 10 kg or 5 kg or polypacks or 1 kg net weight. Again canned foods come in different sizes containing different net weights of foods. Depending on the requirements of individual food service, the appropriate sizes will need to be purchased.

(e) Quantities to be bought of each commodity at a time:

The buying quantities will depend on number of factors:

(i) Degree or perishability of the food and thus its keeping quality.

(ii) Rate of use in the menus of establishments.

(iii) Frequency of deliveries possible.

(iv) Amount of storage space avail be and the types of storages necessary for different foods.

(f) *Suppliers and their terms of supply*: Very often suppliers agreed to fixed prices of a range of items over a period of time and have no objections to supplying immediately on demand. Others may be rigid on the mode of delivery in which case stocks have to be maintained with the establishment. For some commodities the establishment may request for items straight from a farm situated close to the establishment. In that case the price advantage may have to be weighed against storage space and immediate usefulness to capture the fresh quality characteristic in prepared meals.

(g) *What quality is best suited for what use in the production of meals*: This only proves that small leakages if not checked at the point of purchase can change a profitability projected situation to one of loss. Others sources through which similar cost effects can be produced are accepting poor quality of food item, where peels are too thick or seeds too large affecting edible portions obtained from foods. Also processed foods which are not of standard quality such as stale or infested cereal products or defective cans can lead to preparation of food items which have lost their normal portion size, colour or flavour. The kitchen is often held responsible for quality of preparation, forgetting the importance of checking flavour at the receiving point. It stands to reason therefore that if poor quality is received, poor quality is served. This can gradually affect volume of sales and thereby profitability.

(h) *Available kinds of storage space*: The amount of space available for storing foods in an establishment will determine the amounts in terms of pack sizes and numbers to be purchased.

The kinds of storages such as cold or freezer storage, at hand will also affect the range of products that can be bought and stored. On this will depend the number of trips to the market or number of deliveries per week or month?

(i) *Relative keeping quality of different foods*: Different types of food, perishable, semi-and non-perishables require different temperature storages if food quality is to be maintained and loss through deterioration prevented.

(j) *Communication of requirements to the supplier to ensure that the right quality is received in the right form and at the right time*: The best way to communicated food requirements to a suppler are by the use of very accurate word pictures of foods and ingredients. Specifications also includes regarding the dates of delivery, pack sizes and numbers.

Food Buyer

An institutional buyer spends a lot of money on behalf of the establishment and for the customers. He thus bears a heavy responsibility for the well being of both. Every food buyer therefore needs to possess certain qualities to work effectively, such as:

(i) High moral and ethical values, so that he is not influenced by or obligated to suppliers in any way:

(ii) Objectivity in his judgment of quality offered in terms of price and service.

(iii) Loyalty to the institution through devotion to duty, exercising a sense of justice, being open-minded but alert to a seller's psychology and being hard working and patient.

(v) Loyalty to customers in terms of being able to recognize good quality food that is free from adulteration and contamination.

(vi) Accepting food brands that are marked by standardizing

agencies approving their quality such as ISI, FPO or AGMARK in India.

Purchasing Activity

From the above discussion it is clear that purchasing food for an establishment is not a single activity involving exchange of money for food in market, but a series of activities from knowing what to buy and for what end use, to actually getting the food for food preparation. Indicates the activities involved.

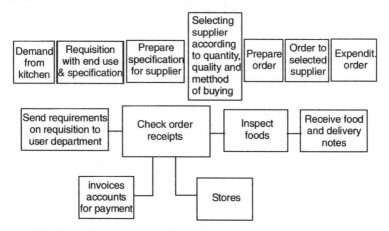

The job of purchasing food becomes even more difficult in countries where there is no system of food grading initiated by the government, which can help the buyer to pick up what is required without any apprehension. However, quality is of utmost concern to all dealing with the preparation, service and consumption of food. Therefore, the consumer had a crucial role to play in establishing quality food and service standards while eating a way from home. He can help to do so by:

(a) Being aware of the dangers of poor quality foods and knowing how to identify desirable quality. The concept of 'acceptable' quality in any food service establishment

171

is really based on what the customer will willingly accept.

(b) Accepting only those meals or foods, which are freshly prepared or finished and served at the right temperatures to ensure microbiological safety.

(c) Visiting only such places where standards of hygiene and sanitation are maintained.

Functions of a Food Buyer

1. To keep records of specifications for each type of dish on the menu developed with the help of those who prepare the meals.

2. Ability to store foods in manner that will enhance or maintain their keeping qualities.

3. Using perishable foods within two days of purchase if used fresh.

4. Rotating use of packaged foods so that older packages are used first.

5. Formulating specifications for foods items.

Buying Food

Every establishment sets its own purchasing policies according to its specific needs for different types of foods. For example, certain establishments may decide to buy their canned and preserved items from government canning centres only.

Others may contact manufactures directly while still others may depend entirely on the supplier's judgments of what would be good. Some establishments may have employees whose families are farming, and their products may be bought farm fresh according to seasonal requirements. Whatever may be the polices laid down, the methods of buying depend largely on the quantities of the various items to be purchased at one time. The different methods possible are discussed below:

Open Market Buying

Most food service establishments use this method for buying food items. The buyer invites quotation from suppliers for items according to required specifications. The supplier is then selected on the basis of his samples, prices, delivery schedule and other services offered. Contact with suppliers is made by visits to markets, on telephone or by visits of sellers to the food service establishment. Open marker buying is an informal method and can easily-be adapted to individual establishments. It is generally used for purchasing of perishable foods like fruits, vegetables, meat, etc. In fact, very small establishments, which are family enterprises often, buy directly from wholesale markets, food stores and cooperatives, and transport, the quantities required to the establishment.

This helps to appreciate and be aware of the changes in market situations and make the best use of prices and commodities by using instant discretion in purchase. For instance, it is not worthwhile for a roadside café to draw up specifications, for the limited menu that it may serve. Therefore, on a visit to the market with an idea of buying brinjal among other vegetables, if the buyer finds that the brinjal are mostly infested and of poor quality, he can instantly decide to replace the item on the menu with a vegetable that is of good quality. Had an order for the same been placed with a supplier, one could land up with a lot of waste because when buying in bulk, say 5 kg, no supplier would pick up perfectly good coloured, well shaped brinjals, to see if some of them have tiny holes.

In larger establishments where suppliers are involved in the purchasing, it helps to use price quotation and order sheets for recording the prices quoted in the time bound contract with a supplier.

Formal Buying

In this method formal quotations are invited from sellers against written specifications for each category of foods. These requests for bids may be made through dailies, or printed material, which is widely distributed or posted to interested sellers who may be contacted on phone. Along with specifications the buyers also included in their requests, conditions like last date for quotation, general time between order and delivery, mode of delivery, terms of payment, willingness to accept whole or part of the bid, discounts, and so on framed within the purchasing policy of each establishment.

The quotations received remain sealed till the date of opening (also indicated in the buyer's requests). They are they opened by the purchasing manager in the presence of the bidders and representatives from the user department, accounts and administrative staff, who witness the quotation accepted.

The Practice is to accept the quotations of the lowest bidder, unless products clearly fail to meet the specifications.

Formal methods of buying are generally adopted by governmental establishments for which central purchasing is done, such as for hospitals, or homes for the handicapped or movement schools. They may also be used for large catering establishments. Formal methods involve a great deal of competitive bidding and therefore are sometimes referred to as 'competitive bid buying

Negotiated Buying

As the name indicates this involves negotiations between buyer and seller regarding prices and quantities. This method is generally used for seasonal items which are limited in supply, where both buyer and seller are keen that the product is lifted quickly and request bids are submitted as soon a possible. Obviously, this method is quicker, more flexible and less formal than the competitive bid method.

Negotiated buying may be adopted when purchasing food items directly from farmers or manufactures but this is generally possible only for very large establishments because the contracts with manufactures would have to for large quantities, e.g. the total farm produce for an item for a season, or one complete manufacturing lot. The advantage is of course in terms of quality as well as price, but storage cost increases. Two types of contracts may be signed between the buyer and seller:

1. A Firm At Opening Price (FAOP) contract: In this the buyer agrees to take the supplies at a price established in the future when yield is known, rather than at per-season prices when the contract is made. Such an agreement is therefore firm but not signed till the seasonal yield is known:
2. A 'Subject to Approval of Price' (SAP) contract: In this case the buyer has the option of rejecting the order if the price fixed in the future is not acceptable to him.

Wholesale Buying

In this method a contract is signed with a wholesaler for purchase of goods at a specific price for a future period. The agreement specifies the intervals between deliveries for the contract period, along with the quantities required and when. This method is also suitable for larger organizations or central purchase departments.

Whatever method is used for purchasing food, it is advisable to make the procedure simple with minimum paper work. Also communicating requirements clearly at all stages of purchasing is vital to the success of any food service \establishment. Some factors, which help food buying, are:

Price: This enables cost comparisons with different brands of similar products to be made instantly, and buying decisions arrived at without undue delay.
Labelling: Labels which indicate quality symbols like ISI, FPO, AGMARK, date of manufacture, expiry date, maximum retail price per kilogram or pack, nutritional information, all enable the food buyer to select foods properly.

Twelve

Revenue Control Systems

In controlling cost for food the control of revenue is equally important in hotel industry.

To control the revenue of a unit, particular attention must be paid to the major factors, which can have an influence on the profitability.

Therefore it is essential to control the main factors which can affect the revenue of a business, such as the menu-beverage sales, the sales mix, the average spend of customers in each selling outlet at different times of the day, the number of covers served and the gross profit margins.

It is important to note, particularly in commercial operations that somewhere in the total control system there is a need for the accountability of what has been served to the customer and the payment for what has been issued from the kitchen or the bar.

The payment for food and beverage may be made in many forms such as cash, foreign currency, credit cards, cheques, travellers' cheques, luncheon type vouchers and signed bills.

All staff handling cash should be adequately trained in the respective company's methods. It is a common practice for a cashier's or waiter's handbook/manual to be produced so that an established procedure may be followed with the specific aim of ensuring that cash security is efficiently carried out at all times. A typical handbook/manual would contain information on the standard procedure to be followed for such things as:

1. *Opening procedure*—Instructions here would include procedures about checking the float, having a float of specific denominations, checking the till roll, recording waiters bill pad numbers, etc.
2. *Working procedure*—Instructions on how to accept payment and the procedure to follow.
3. *Closing procedure*—Instructions on any documentation and recordings to be completed, cashing up, recording of credit cards, cheques, etc.
4. *Procedure for accepting foreign currency*—what currency is to be accepted, how to obtain the current exchange rates, how this is to be recorded, etc.
5. *Procedure for accepting credit cards*—which credit cards are to be accepted, how they are to be checked, method of processing credit cards for payment, recording of credit vouchers, etc.
6. *Procedures for accepting vouchers such as luncheon vouchers*—which vouchers are acceptable, how this is to be recorded.
7. *Procedure for accepting cheques*—how cheques are to be made out, customers to produce a valid cheque guarantee card, checking that signatures correspond, etc.
8. *Procedure for accepting travellers' cheques*—what travellers' cheques are acceptable, what currencies are acceptable, witnessing and checking signatures, how this is to be recorded.
9. Procedure for a complimentary or signed bill-check against current list of authorized persons and their signature, how this is to be recorded.

There are two basic approaches to recording and controlling food and beverage sales.

1. *A manual system*, which is commonly used in small and in exclusive type catering units.
2. *An automated system*, which is commonly used in units with several outlets, in units with a very high volume of business and in up-to-date companies with may units.

Manual System

One of the simplest steps to take when attempting to establish sales control procedures is to require that each item ordered and its selling price are recorded on a waiter's sales check. Using some form of a check system serves the following functions:

1. To remind the waiting staff of the order they have taken.
2. To give a record of sales so that portion sales and sale mixes and sales histories can be compiled.
3. To assist the cashier and facilitate easy checking of prices charged.
4. To show the customer a detailed list of charges made.

An additional aid is to use numbered checks and control these tightly, recording all cancelled and missing checks.

It is more common to find duplicate or triplicate checks being used as an aid to control for the following reasons:

1. They provide the kitchen, buffet, or bar with a written record of what has been ordered and issued.
2. They authorize the kitchen, buffet, or bar to issue the food and/or beverage.
3. They provide the opportunity to compare the top copy of the check with the duplicate to ensure that all that has been issued has been charged and paid for.

In addition to following precisely the unit's procedure for the handling of all revenue transactions within the restaurant or bars, it is normal practice for the cashier working a manual system to be required to complete the following:

1. To issue check pads to the waiting staff prior to a meal period, to record the numbers of the checks issued in each pad, and obtain the checks issued in each pad, and obtain the waiting staff's signature for them, and on the completion of the meal period to receive from the waiting staff their respective unused check pads, record the numbers, and sign for the receipt of those returned. These information to be recorded on the check number issue control sheet.

2. To check the pricing, extensions and subtotals charges and to entire the total amount due.

3. To receive and check money, credit or, when applicable, an approved signature in payment for the total amount due for each check.

4. To complete the missing check list for each meal period. This is an aid to the cashier in controlling what checks are used. The respective check numbers on the list are crossed out when payment is made. When a missing check is identified, investigation to be carried out to find the reason for this and if no satisfactory explanation is forthcoming, to inform a member of management on duty. Missing checks to be marked on the missing checklist.

5. To complete the restaurant sales control sheet for each meal period. This form requires that all revenue received (such as cash, cheques, credit card transactions, etc.). From this control sheet basic data-such as the number of covers served or the average spends per customer on food an beverage—is quickly obtained.

6. To complete the necessary paying in of all cash, etc. in accordance with the unit's established practice. This could

be direct to a bank whether a mall independent unit, or a unit of a large company, or to the head cashier's office if a large unit with many outlets. An example of a daily banking and till control sheet.

Problems of the manual system

In brief, the basic problems of controlling any food and beverage operation are:

1. The time spend between purchasing, receiving, storing, processing, selling the product, and obtaining the cash or credit for the product, is sometimes only a few hours.
2. The number of items (food and beverage) held in stock at any time is high.
3. A large number of finished items are produced from a combination of the large number of items held in stock.
4. The number of transactions taking place on an hourly basis in some operations can be very high.
5. To be able to control the operation efficiently, management ideally requires control in formation of many types to be available quickly and to be presented in a meaningful way.

The full manual control of a food and beverage operation would be costly, time consuming and data produced would frequently be far too late for meaningful management action to take place. Certain aspects of control such as regularly up-dating the costing of standard recipes, calculating gross profit potentials, and providing detailed sales analysis would seldom be done because of the time and labour involved.

A manual system providing a restricted amount of basis data is still widely used in small-and medium-sized units although they are likely to be replaced in the near future by machine or electronic systems.

The day-to-day operational problems of a manual system are many and include such common problems as:

1. Poor handwriting by waiting staff resulting in:

    (a) Incorrect order given to the kitchen or dispense bar:
    (b) Wrong food being offered to the customer.
    (c) Incorrect prices being charged to the customer.
    (d) Poorly presented bill for the customer, etc.

2. Human error can produce such mistakes as:

    (a) Incorrect prices charged to items on a bill
    (b) Incorrect additions to a customer's bill.
    (c) Incorrect service charge made.
    (d) Incorrect government tax (for example VAT) charge made.

3. The communication between departments such as the restaurant, dispense bar, kitchen and cashiers has to be done physically by the waiting staff going costly to produce.

5. Manual systems have to be restricted to the bare essentials because of the high cost of labour that would be involved in providing detailed up-to-date information.

Machine System

Pre-checking Systems

Pre-check machines are somewhat similar in appearance to a standard cash register and are designed to operate only when a sales check is inserted into the printing table to the side of the machine.

The machine is operated in the following way:

1. A waiter jobs his/her own machine key.
2. A check is inserted into the printing table and the particular

keys, depending on the order taken, are pressed giving an item and price record as well as recording the table number, the number of covers and the waiter's reference number.

3. A duplicate is printed and issued by the machine, which is then issued as the duplicate check to obtain food and/or beverages.

4. For each transaction a reference number is given on the sales check and the duplicate.

5. All data is recorded on a continuous audit tape that can be removed only by authorized persons at the end of the day when the machine is cleared and total sales taken and compared to actual cash received.

The advantages of the system are:

1. The sales check is made out and a record of it made on the audit tape before the specific items can be obtained from the kitchen or bar.

2. Analysis of total sales per waiter is made on the audit tape at the end of each shift.

3. No cashier is required as each waiter acts as his/her own cashier, each keeping the cash collected from customers until the end of the shift and then paying it in.

4. As each waiter has his/her own security key to operate the machine, there is strict assess to the machines and no other way by which per-checks can be provided and used in exchange for items from the kitchen or bar.

Pre-set pre-checking system

This is an up-date on the basic per-check machine. The keyboard is much larger than the previous machines, and has descriptive keys corresponding to all items on the menu which are pre-set to the current price of each item. A waiter pressing the key for, say one cheeseburger would not only have the item printed out but also the price. A control panel, kept under lock and key, would enable management to change the price of any item, if required and at the end of a meal period by depressing each key in turn to get a print out giving a basic analysis of sales made.

These are very high speed machines, which were developed mainly for operations such as supermarkets and were further adapted for use in high volume catering operations show a customer's bill produced on an ECR. The particular advantages of these machines are that they will:

1. Price customers' checks through pre-set or by price look-ups.
2. Print checks, including the printing of previously entered items.
3. Have an additional special key so that the present price can be changed during promotional periods such as happy hour in bar.
4. Provide an analysis of sales made by type of product and if required by hour (or other similar period) of trading.
5. Provide an analysis of sales by waiter per hour or per shift period.
6. Analyse sales by method of payment, for example cash, cheque, type of credit card, etc.
7. Complete automatic tax calculations and cover and service changes.
8. Provide some limited stock control.
9. Provide waiter checking in and checking out facilities.
10. Provide facilities for operator training to take place on the machine without disrupting any information already in the ECR.
11. Restrict access to the ECR and the till drawer by the key or code for each operator.

12. Have rotating turret displays of prices charged to individual customer transactions This is of particular value in self-service and counter operations.
13. Eliminate the need for a cashier, by requiring each waiter to be responsible for taking payment from the customers and paying in the exact amount as recorded by the ECR at the end of each shift.

Electronic cash registers are not without their problems and it is important to consider the following prior to selecting an ECR for purchase.

1. It is suitable for the type and size of operation it is to be used in?
2. Cost—how does this compare with other models of similar capacity?
3. Is it an up-to-data model or is it about to be superseded?
4. What on-site training will be offered if this model is purchased?
5. Can this ECR be linked to similar ECRs as part of a network or directly to a microcomputer?
6. Maintenance. How foolproof is this machine?
   What level of maintenance is normally expected? Can staff do simple maintenance, for example, changing of the printing ribbon, etc.?
7. What safeguards (for example, battery override) are standard or optional to the model when power failures occur (The memory of the day's business could be lost in a power failure causing a serious loss of control.)
8. What built-in security features are included so as to restrict access to commands, re-setting, and disclosure of information to authorized personnel?
9. Will this particular model of ECR function perfectly when near to other powerful electrical equipment?
10. Does this model of ECR have a seal-in keyboard to restrict

dust and moisture, which could result in the keys of the ECR operating intermittently?

Point-of-sale control systems

At a basic level a point-of-sale control system is no more than a modern ECR with the additional feature of one or several printers at such locations as the kitchen (or sections of the kitchen) or dispense bar. Some systems replace the ECR with a 'server terminal' (also called 'waiter communication' systems), which may be placed at several locations within a restaurant, and is a modification of an ECR in that the cash features are eliminated making the terminal relatively small and inconspicuous.

1. To provide an instant and separate clear and printed order to the kitchen or bar, of what is required and by and for whom.
2. To speed up the process of giving the order to the kitchen or bar.
3. To aid control, in that items can only be ordered when they have been entered into the ECR or terminal by an identifiable member of the waiting staff and printed.
4. To reduce the time taken by the waiter in walking to the kitchen or bar to place an order and, as frequently happens, to check if an order is ready for collection.
5. To afford more time, if required, for customer contact.

Printers are at time replaced by VDU screens. Server terminals are part of a computer-based point-of-sale system. These special terminals are linked to other server terminals in the restaurants and bars within one system and, if required to, also interface with other systems so that, for example, the transfer of restaurant and bar charges may be made via the front office computer system. The advantage of a computerized point-of-sales system is that it is capable of processing data as activities occur, which makes it possible to obtain up-to-the minute reports for management who can be better informed and able to take immediate and accurate corrective action if necessary.

This type of point-of-sale control system has been taken one step further with the introduction of hand-held terminals. Remanco's electronic server pad (ESP), for example, is a palm-size unit, which uses radio frequencies to communicate from the guest's table direct to the kitchen and bar preparation areas. The use of such a terminal offers a number of advantages: food and beverage orders are delivered faster and more efficiently to preparation sites; waiters in turn can attend more tables; with a two-way communication service staff can be notified if an item is out of stock; all food and beverage items ordered are immediately charged to the guest's bill which is accurate and easy to read finally operations can reassess their labour utilization and efficiency, certain members of the services staff, for example, can take the simple orders, while others can spend more time with customers to increase food and beverage sales.

The ESP is a completely noiseless terminal with orders being entered alphabetically, numerically or by using pre-set codes. When not being used and the unit is closed, its design resembles a conventional order pad, compact and light in weight that can easily be carried around by service staff, it is currently being utilised in a variety of situations, including restaurants; coffee shops; and in lounge areas.

Microcomputers

Before the invention of the microprocessor only a few large organizations were able to justify the high cost of a computer system. In the hotel and catering industry these system were mainly applied to areas such as the front office, a including purchasing, storing, stock control, standard recipes, menu planning, pricing, sales analysis, etc. received scant attention from computer firms.

The information required by food and beverage management, to be efficient, is demanding in terms of computer programming, storage and retrieval of data. The move from manual systems, to systems aided by mechanical cash registers, to systems aided by the many types of ECRs, has led to the evolution of totally computer-aided control systems.

The reason for this evolution is simply that the computer equipment necessary for a food and beverage control system is getting smaller, more powerful, cheaper, more reliable, less complicated for an operator to use, and relevant software packages are available. The requirement is of two kinds:

1. *Hardware*: The physical unit of computer unit includes VDU, printers and hard disk drives.
2. *Software*: The computer programmes designed and written to fulfil a specific purpose.

From the user's perspective, software's seem as being in two major categories:

(i) *Packages*—software that is bought in from a computer firm and is already pre-programmed to perform a specific function, for example payroll, stock control, etc.
(ii) *User-developed programs*—software that is designed by the food and beverage management staff or by company staff with or without the assistance of computer programming expertise.

In addition, computer firms are marketing turnkey systems, which are pre-programmed software packages designed to serve a particular sector of the industry or to perform a particular function; they may also come with the necessary hardware. The basis of this marketing approach is that it would be far too expensive to purchase computer hardware and then employ computer-programming staff to write a specific set of programs for a unit or company.

The problem with total packages and systems is that they will have been prepared for a very general market so as to be of a wide appeal, and a generalist approach to solving a problem or presenting data will have been taken. With the diversified nature of the hotel and catering industry and the highly personal manner in which many business are operated, many of the packages are not entirely acceptable. However, turn key systems and some carefully selected packages are being successfully used, particularly in the small-to medium-sized operations and companies where often the menu size and ingredients used are not that large and also when a significant used are not that large and also when a significant proportion of the food purchased is of the pre-prepared and pre-packaged kind. At this point it is significant for the reader to identify both those large and small companies who have a total and efficient computerized food and beverage control system as well as those companies who are still realign very much on a mixture of a manual system enhanced with ECRs.

The cost of a computerized system would include:

1. The system hardware.
2 The system software
3. The cost of additional or special programming.
4. The cost of training staff and payroll costs.
5. The cost of running a dual system whilst the new system run-in and initial problems ironed out.
6. The cost of maintenance which should be by contract whenever possible.
7. The cost of supplies, for example computer paper, etc.

Careful planning is necessary by an organization prior to selecting the hardware and software best suited to its needs from the wide range of models and packages available. The following steps should be taken to ensure that the most suitable system is purchased.

1. Analyse the present system for its strengths and weaknesses. By careful analysis determine exactly what the information requirements are for all areas of the organization's operation and management.
2. In general terms summarize the equipment specifications by reference to the information requirements.
3. Select a list of potential suppliers and request literature. Follow this with a request of a presentation of their equipment and if still interested ask for a full demonstration.
4. Obtain from a short list of potential suppliers full details of companies using their equipment and packages. Visit some of these companies and talk to the management and the operators.
5. Check if the programs are simple to understand in that the operator is continually guided through the system with unambiguous prompting on the VDU screen. In addition, that well prepared training manuals are included with the equipment.
6. Check if the supplier can modify the software packages to the particular requirements of the organization.
7. Conduct a financial analysis of alternative short-listed suppliers' equipment and select a supplier.
8. Have the system put into full operation with the suppliers' training and technical staff standing by to assist with initial problems as they occur. If an existing control system is in operation, this should be continued for a period until the new system is working correctly and all staff training fully completed.

The advantages of a carefully selected microcomputer—based information system for a catering operation are in its ability to provide for management's easy and quick access to accurate and complete information related to the total (or part of the) business at any time that it is required, thus allowing management more time to evaluate the information produced and take action quickly when required.

Operating yardsticks used in controlling

Besides the general operating ratios that have been used earlier in this chapter, for example food cost in relation to food sales, beverage cost in relation to beverage shale's, etc., there are many more that are used and found to be of value. The following is a brief explanation of those that are frequently used.

Total food and beverage sales

The total food and beverage sales should be recorded, checked and measured against the budgeted sales figures for the particular period (for example week or month).

The analysis of these figures is usually done daily for large establishments and for those that are not operating a manual control system. The analysis would show separately the food sales and the beverage sales per outlet and per meal period.

The importance of this yardstick cannot be emphasized enough other than to remind the reader that it is cash and cash only that can be banked and not percentages or any ratio or factor figures.

Departmental Profit

Departmental profit is calculated by deducting the departmental expenses from the departmental sales, the expenses being the sum of the cost of food and beverages sold, the cost of labour and the cost of overheads charged against the department, and the profit being usually expressed as a percentage of the departmental sales, for example:

$$\text{Department profit } (1,200) \times \frac{100}{1} = 15\%$$

Food and beverage sales (8,000)

The departmental profit should be measured against the budget figures for that period.

Ratio of Food/Beverage Sales to Total Sales

It is worthwhile for food and beverage sales to be separated from each other and to express each of them as a percentage of the total sales. This would be a measure of performance against the established standard budgeted percentage as well as indicating general trends in the business.

Average Spending Power

This measures the relationship between food sales and beverage sales to the number of customers served. If food sales are 350 and the number of customers is 5. The average spending power (ASP) for beverages is usually related to the number of items recorded on the till roll, rather than to the number of customers, and the total beverage sales. Thus if 600 is the recorded beverage sales and an analysis of the till roll showed that 400 drinks had been sold, the average spend per drink would be 1.50. What is different here is that a customer may order several drinks during an evening and therefore the average amount spent on a drink is more important than the ASP per customer. To calculate the ASP for bottled wine sales in a restaurant or at a banquet though could be a useful exercise.

Sales Mix

This measures the relationship between the various components of the total sales of a unit, for example:

Sales mix	%
Coffee shop sales	
food	20
Beverage	5
Restaurant sales	
food	25
beverages	15
Banqueting sales	
food	20
beverages	10
Cocktail bar sales	
beverage	5
	200

In addition, a sales mix may be calculated for the food and beverage menus for each outlet under group headings such as appetizers, main course items, sweet course, coffees, etc.; and spirits, cocktails, beers etc. This would not only highlight the most and least popular items, but would at times help to explain a disappointing gross profit percentage that the reason often being that each item is usually costs at different gross profit percentages and if the customers are choosing those items with a low gross profit this would result in the overall gross profit figure being less than budgeted for.

Payroll Costs

Payroll costs are usually expressed as a percentage of sales and are normally higher, the higher the level of service offered. It is vital that they are tightly controlled as they contribute a high percentage of the total costs of running an operation.

Establishing a head count of employees per department, or establishing the total number of employee hours allowed per department in relation to a known average volume of business can control payroll costs. In addition, all overtime must be strictly controlled and should only be permitted when absolutely necessary.

The index of productivity can be calculated separately for food sales, beverage sales or for total food and beverage sales.

The use of the term payroll costs in the formula includes not only the appropriate payroll costs, but also any other employee benefits such as employers' pension contributions, medical insurance, etc.

The index of productivity would vary depending on the type of operation, for example a fast food restaurant with a take-away service would have a high index of productivity, as the payroll costs would be lower than a luxury restaurant employing highly skilled and expensive staff with a high ratio of staff to customers, which may have a relatively low index of productivity.

As payroll cost can be controlled and should be related to the forecasted volume of business, a standard index of productivity can be established to measure how accurately the two elements are related.

Stock turnover

It is calculated by the formula: The rate of stock turnover gives the number of times that the average level of stock has turned over in a given period.

Too high a turnover would indicate very low levels of stocks being held and a large number of small value purchases being made. This is costly and time consuming for whoever does the purchasing as well as costly for the purchases as no price advantage can be taken of the standard quantity offers made by suppliers. Too low a turnover would indicate unnecessary capital tied up in an operation and therefore additionally a larger control and security problem.

This shows the sales value that can be earned by each seat in a restaurant, coffee shop, etc. As in section 16,4.10, the seat is the selling point and is required to contribute a certain value to turnover and profits.

Rate of seat turnover

This shows the number of times that each seat in a restaurant, coffee shop, etc. is used by customers during a specific period. Thus, if in a 120 seater coffee shop 400 customers were served in a three-hour lunch period, the rate of seat turnover would be 400 divided by 120, that is, 3.33. As the coffee shop staff can only sell food to customers while they are seated at a table, the importance of the rate of seat turnover is highlighted.

Sales per waiter/waitress

Each waiter/waitress will have a known number of covers for which he/she is responsible. This would vary depending on the style of food and beverage service offered. As salespeople for the restaurant or coffee shop, their takings should be of a predetermined target level so as to contribute to a satisfactory level of turnover and profit.

Sales per square foot/metre^2

This is self-explanatory in that the space of all selling outlets needs to be used to its best advantage so as to achieve a desired turnover and profit. This can be calculated on a square foot/ metre basis. As the square footage per customer varies with the type of food and beverage service offered, so must the costs to the customer so that an establishment is earning the desired turnover and profit per square foot of selling space.

Thirteen

Book Keeping and Accounting

Every food service establishment needs to be assessed periodically to determine its state efficiency. This assessment is greatly facilitated if accurate books of account are maintained for all transactions that take place. The process of recording transactions is referred to as book keeping or record keeping. The preparation of statements for assessing the state of profitability and their interpretation for guiding decisions regarding the operations of the business are considered as accounting functions.

Book Keeping

A number of transactions both gig and small take place in a food service establishment. A purchase of equipment worth of Rs 5,000 or the purchase of stationary worth of Rs 5 are both equally important transaction. A systematic record of all large and small transactions is essential. If the establishment is involved with an outsider in any event, the event becomes a business transaction provided it is measurable in terms of money. The largest numbers of transactions in a business are of the type in which outsiders are involved. Thus the major part of the records of a food service establishment will be with reference to transactions with others.

In addition to these there are a number of transactions that are not directly concerned with individuals such as loss due to fire, wear and tear of the equipment, etc. It is essential that such transactions should also be recorded.

Transactions need to be recorded in such a way that a clear and accurate picture emerges of the state of the business at any time. Book keeping is therefore essentially a method adopted to record transactions, based on a well thought of and effective system.

As all transactions have to be recorded in monetary terms, this implies a transfer of money or money's worth value or benefit. When salaries are paid the employees are receiving the benefit and the employer is giving the benefit. It can be said that all business transactions have two aspects giving the benefit and receiving the benefit.

Systems of Book Keeping

There are two systems of book keeping, the single entry system and the double entry system. The single entry system is not strictly speaking a system, as it is not based on sound principles. Some transactions are not recorded whereas there is only a partial record for others and reliable results cannot therefore be obtained.

The double entry system is more soundly based on the concept that all transactions involve giving and receiving a benefit. This system provides for an accurate and complete record of both aspects of all transactions in an establishment. For example if provisions are purchased the stock of provisions will increase and either the cash in hand or cash in the bank will be recorded, or an obligation to pay the price at a later date will be created. Fundamentally the record of transactions must recognize both the aspects of giving and receiving the benefit or value, if it is to be a proper and useful record. This is what is done under the double entry system.

Further, the two aspects of business transactions may relate to any two or one of the following main elements:

1. Persons or firms Properties
2. Expenses or income

If equipment is to be purchased for cash the two aspects of the transactions are, the incoming equipment and the outgoing cash. If the rent of a building is received, cash received is an aspect. If salaries are paid in cash, salaries indicate one-aspect and a cash payment indicates the other. If cash is received from debtor, and the cash received is one aspect and the debtor who is paying the cash is the other important aspect to be recorded. In this way the two aspects of every transactions can be picked out of the above three elements. So far as one aspect relates to a person or firm it has to be ascertained whether the person or firm is a receiver or giver. If the aspect relates to properties it may indicate whether the property is coming in or going out.

Lastly an aspect of the transactions may be concerned with either an expense or an income. Thus it is apparent that:

1. Firms or persons may be either receivers or givers
2. Properties may either come in or go out
3. A transactions may be either expense or an income

It may be noted that each of the above elements has two parts that have to be recorded. In order to have a systematic record each element will need to be recorded independently. Firms or persons will be provided with independent pages divided vertically in two parts a debit side and credit side.

The amount will be written on the debit side if the person or firm is a receiver and it will be written on the credit side of a firm or person is a giver. Similarly each property will be recorded on an independent page. Thus whenever a property comes in it will be recorded on the debit side and income on the credit side. In all accounts the debit side is the left side and the credit is on the right hand side of every page.

Accounts

When all transactions relation to one person are set out in one page, it is known as a 'Personal Account' showing transactions in debt and credit form. Similarly, when all transactions are pertaining to one property, it is termed as a 'Real Account'. For example Cash Book or Cash Account. In the same way, when expenses and incomes are recorded independently on separate pages, they are known as 'Nominal accounts'.

Thus the rules regarding double entry book-keeping system can be summed up as follows:

(a) Personal Accounts:
   (i) Debit the receiver,
   (ii) Credit the giver.
(b) Real Account:
   (i) Debit what comes in,
(c) Nominal Account:
   (i) Debit all expenses and losses.
   (ii) Credit all incomes and gains.

All book keeping records will be based on these principles.

Advantages of the Double Entry System

The double entry system of book keeping has a number of advantages:

1. An establishment can know whenever it wants how much profit it has earned, or how much it has suffered in a particular period. This information is essential to ascertain whether the business is being run on the right path or whether it needs correction.

2. The precise reasons leading to profit or loss can be ascertained and necessary remedial action taken well in time.

3. It is possible to prepare a balance sheet at the end of a trading period, disclosing the financial state of affairs during that period it will be known whether the firm is solvent or insolvent. Moreover a comparative study of different years can be undertaken to ascertain the progress of the operation.

4. As the business firm can know at any moment, the amount owing from debtors and the amounts owing to creditors it can arrange to send reminders to the debtors who fail to pay in time, and reduce chances of bad debts. At the same time a strict, which can be kept on the creditors so that the firm knows what amount is to be paid and when.

5. Accurate record of transactions is assured under the double entry system, as the existence of errors is revealed by the preparation of the Trial Balance a list of the balances of all the accounts.

6. Through this system not only are errors prevented but any frauds can also be discovered and prevented.

7. Management can be guided in decision making through properly kept accounts.

8. From the tax point of view, the figures of profit provided by the double entry system are accepted by tax authorities.

The double entry system can be adopted even by non-profit making organization, like old age homes, school hostel, etc. with equal advantage.

Book of Account

The transaction of a food service establishment fall into three main categories:

1. Receipt and payments of cash, including payments and withdrawals from a bank account.
2. Purchases of goods, materials and stores.
3. Sale of goods and services.

There will be one book to record cash and bank transactions, another to record credit purchase of goods and third to record the credit sale of goods. If there is any other category of recurring transactions a separate book can be maintained for that also.

Thus the following books are initially kept to record the transactions of different categories:

1. *Cash book* for recording cash receipt and payments including those for cash purchases, expenses incurred cash sales discounts allowed and discounts received. The cash book has both debit and credit column.
2. *Purchase book* for recording all goods purchased on credit.
3. *Sales book* for recording all goods sold on creditors.
4. *Purchase returns book* for recording all purchases returned to suppliers, that is creditors.
5. *Sales returns* book for recording all sales returned by the customers. This book of account is generally not required in catering establishments, because food sold or taken away from the establishment is never returned.
6. *Journal* for recording all those transactions for which there is no specific book maintained. Of all the books of account, the cash book forms part of the double entry system of book-keeping and is maintained on the basis of the principles already discussed. All other books are the auxiliary books of original entry and are simply an aid to recording these transactions further into the principle book of account, the ledger. All the entries in the ledger are

made according to the double entry system, recording them both as debit and credit entries.

Cash Book

This book is kept in order to maintain the daily record of transactions relating to receipts and payments of cash. As the number of transactions relating to cash is usually large and there is risk of cash being unaccounted, it is necessary to maintain up-to-date cash records, which are properly supervised. The Cash Book is maintained based on the principles of the double entry system, and it involves the record of transactions relating to a property (cash). All receipts will be recorded on the debit side (what comes in), and all payments will be recorded on the credit side (what goes out).

Single Column Cash Book

This is a simple cash book which is ruled with a single 'amount' column on each side as shown in the figure.

Single Cash Book

Receipts							Payments
Debit							Credit
Date	Particulars	L.F.	Amount Rs. P.	Date	Particular	L.F.	Amount Rs. P.

Double Column Cash Book

This is known as the Discount Column Cash Book. In addition to the two amount columns on each side a discount column is also added to each amount column. Usually a cash discount is allowed to customers who pay promptly. Similarly, the suppliers also allow discount when prompt payment is made to them.

Cash discount accompanies cash receipts from customers and payments to suppliers. It is therefore convenient to record discount allowed or received along with cash payment. The discount allowed (loss) on receipt of cash from a customer will, according to the principles of double entry, be recorded in the discount column on the debt side, and the discount received (gain) on payment to the supplier will be recorded on the credit side in the discount column. Figure is a sample of the Double Column Cash Book.

Double Column Cash Book

Receipts									Payments
Debit									Credit
Date	Particulars	L.F.	Discount	Amount	Date	Particular	L.F.	Discount	Amount

Triple Column Cash Book Or Bank Column Cash Book

Today, in almost all establishments, transactions are made through the banks rather than in cash. Organisations prefer to keep cash in the bank rather than on the premises due to various reasons. Moreover, money in the bank is as good as cash. Under these circumstances therefore, it is advantageous to have a column for bank transactions along with the other two columns of the cash book, on both the debt and the credit side. These columns will record all payments made into the bank and all amounts withdrawn from it, in the same manner as the cash receipts and payments are recorded. With the addition of a bank column on each side, there will be three columns on each side of the cash book and therefore it is known as the Triple Column Cash Book.

As explained above, the cash will be entered on the debit side (cash column) and the payments of cash on the credit side (cash column).

Cheques issued by the organisation represent payments out of the bank and hence the amounts will be entered in the bank column on the credit side. When cash or cheques are paid into the bank account, the amounts represent receipts into the bank and will therefore be entered in the bank column on the debit side. Cheques received by the establishment should be entered in the bank column straightway because the cheques have to be sent to the bank for collection and clearance.

When cash is withdrawn from the bank for use it should be entered in the cash column (debit side), and it must at the same time be entered in the bank column on the credit side indicating that the cash has been withdrawn from the bank and the used. Similarly, if cash is deposited into the bank, the amount is entered in the bank column (debit side) and in the cash column (credit side). As these entries are made simultaneously on both debit and credit sides of the cash book they are known as 'contra entries'. In order to indicate this feature of these transactions, the letter 'C' indicating 'contra' is written in the ledger folio (L.F.) column on both sides. This means that the double entry for these transactions is completed in the cash book itself. Discount columns will continue to be used in the same way, whether it is a payment out of the bank or cash, or whether it is a receipt of cash or a cheque.

The two columns, that is, the bank and cash columns would be balanced separately. The total of the cash column (debit side) will always be bigger than the total of the cash column (credit side), and there than will always be a debit balance. On the other hand, the total of the bank column (debit side) is usually bigger than the total of the bank column (credit side), and generally there is a debit balance, but it can be the other way round, when the bank account is over drawn. In that cash the credit total of the bank column will be larger than the corresponding debit total indicating that the bank account has been overdrawn. This shows that the payments have exceeded the amount in the bank. The balance of both these columns are than carried forward to the next period.

Posting of Cash Book

As discussed earlier, each transaction has two important aspects to be recorded under the double entry system of book-keeping. One aspect of each transaction is recorded in the cash book on the credit side system of book-keeping. One aspect of each transaction is recorded in the cash book on the credit side for some transactions, and on the debit side for the other transactions. For contra transactions, both the aspects are recorded. In order to complete the double entry record, another aspect is recorded in the individual accounts to be opened in another book known as the 'ledger'. The particulars column on the debit side of the cash book indicates the account in which the money has been received.

These accounts are opened in the ledger and credited with the respective amounts. Similarly, the particulars column on the credit side indicates the accounts in which the amounts have been paid. All such accounts are debited in the ledger. In case a person or an organisation has paid some amount and discount has been allowed (as shown in the discount column), his account in the ledger must be credited with the total of the amount, including discount received from him. Similarly, if an amount has been paid, to an individual or organisation and some discount has been received, their accounts must be debited with amount including discount. The total of the discount column on the debit side (loss), is posted on the debit side of the discount account and the total of the credit side discount column (gain) should be posted to the credit side of the discount account in the ledger. Items marked 'C' need not be posted because their double entry aspect is already complete in all respects in the cash book itself.

This book is maintained in order to make a preliminary record of the good purchased on credit from the suppliers. There is no record in the form of debits or credits. It is merely a memorandum book. After a Purchase Book is prepared and totalled, it is posted according to the principles of the double entry system. The suppliers being the 'givers', their accounts will be credited with the amounts.

The total of the Purchase Book will be posted to the debit side of the Purchases Account at the end of a particular period, as it represents the expenses incurred on purchases, and expenses are always debited according to the double entry system.

Sales Book

This is maintained in order to record and credit sale of goods to customers during a particular period. This is also a memorandum book and there are no debit and credit columns in it. The total of this book represents total credit sales made to customers. The total, therefore, will be credited (being the receivers of benefit) will be debited in the ledger. In this way, with the help of the basic records in separated books, the double entry records will be complete.

The formats for the Purchase Book and the Sales Book are given in Figures respectively.

205

Purchases Book
Date Particulars L.F. Details Amount
Rs.   Rs.
Total _____

Sales Book
Date Particulars L.F. Details Amount
Rs.   Rs.
Total _____

Purchase Return Book

This is also a memorandum book and records the return of goods to the suppliers. The format of this book is similar to that of the Purchase Book. While posting, the total of this book will be posted to the Returns Outward Account and the supplier's individual accounts will be debited, he being the receiver of the value.

Sales Return Book

The returns from customers are recorded in this book on a memorandum basis. It has already been mentioned that in catering establishments there is practically no occasion for customers to return the product since it is consumable generally on the premises. In establishments which offer a takeaway service, there may be a single instance when the food is brought back with a complaint. In such cases even, it is general practice to replace the item with a fresh one for the customer, therefore such stray occasions do not warranty the necessity to maintain a separate Sales Return Book. It is, however, useful to know that this account book too is not part of the double entry system, but helps to complete a double entry record if returns do take place frequently. Perhaps in establishments, which sell packaged goods or provisions in addition to running a coffee shop, this book would also help to determine the quality of goods to stock. Those items, which are being returned too frequently, can thus be deleted from the purchase list.

The total of the Sales Return Book is recorded on the debit side of the Sales Return or Return Inwards Account and the individual customer's accounts are credited with the amounts of the goods returns. The ruling of this book is the same as that of the Sales Book

Journal

There are certain transactions which cannot be recorded either in the Cash Book, Sales Book, Purchase Book, or the Purchases Return book or the Sales Return Book, neither can these be recorded in any subsidiary book. Such transactions are credit purchase and sales of assets, bad debts, depreciation on assets, outstanding expenses and income earned but not yet received, etc. In order to make an initial record of such transactions a book known as the Journal is maintained. This book records an analysis of every transaction that takes place in an establishment. It states the two accounts, which are involved in the transaction and which one has to be debited and which to be credited. At the end of a given period, the various accounts involved in the transactions are posted with the help of the journal entries.

Entries in the journal are recorded on the basis of the double entry system. Figure illustrates the manner in which the pages of the Journal area set out.

Trial Balance

Once all the transactions are recorded in various account books, it is necessary to check their accuracy by preparing a statement known as the Trial Balance. This lists the balances of all the accounts in debit and credit from. As each transaction had been entered twice, both in debit and credit, the total of the two sides should be equal. The equality of the totals will prove that the accounts have been correctly prepared while preparing the Trial

Balance, the personal and real (property) accounts are balanced, and the amounts of the nominal accounts are noted against each item in the respective column. With the help of a Trail balance, which is prepared at the end of a financial year, the profit or loss for the year and Balance Sheet can be determined as on that date. In fact, with the Trial Balance for the month, the profit or loss for the month can also be calculated. Trail Balance of the restaurant being discussed will appear as follows:

Profit and Loss Account

If the Trial Balance is analysed, we find that items appearing on the debit side represent nominal expenses, properties (Cash and furniture) and personal accounts of debtors (form whom amounts are due, like M/s Modern School). On the credit side there are items representing incomes (sales, etc.) and personal accounts of creditors, along with the capital account.

In order to find out profit or loss, expenses are matched with the incomes. Therefore while preparing the profit and loss account, to real accounts and personal accounts will not be taken into consideration.

These are taken into account at the time of preparing the balance sheet. Real accounts are all assets. Personal accounts representing debtors (with debit balances) are treated as assets, and those personal accounts with credit balance (creditors and capital accounts) are treated as liabilities. Profit or loss shown by the Profit and Loss Account is added or deducted (as the case may be) to from the Capital Account in the Balance Sheet.

In conclusion it can be said that, irrespective of the size of an establishment it is important to maintain a full set of account books accurately in order to ascertain the viability of the operation.

Through the Trial Balance, which can be prepared at any time during the year, the accuracy of the accounts can be maintained. The Profit and Loss Account gives the profitability situation at any time desired. The Balance Sheet projects the present financial position of the establishment in terms of its assets and liabilities. This can guide future plans for investments in fixed assets and help in the provision of necessary working capital.

Index